Leaves From Life, by L.N.R

LEAVES

FROM

LIFE

BY

L.N.R.

LONDON
SAMUEL BAGSTER & SONS
PATERNOSTER ROW

LEAVES FROM LIFE.

BY

L. N. R.

AUTHOR OF "THE BOOK AND ITS STORY."

LONDON:

SAMUEL BAGSTER AND SONS,

15, PATERNOSTER ROW.

———

M.DCCC.LV.

PREFACE.

THESE Leaves from Life, with a few Blossoms inter-
twined, are memorials of simple incidents and records of
feelings, common at one time or another to most individuals, and to ordinary family circles. The histories of
peaceful homes abound in touches of the poetical, amid
much plain prose; and we all desire now and then to
express and embody some domestic experiences, which
would otherwise be forgotten.

In arranging these pieces, composed at considerable
intervals, they have fallen naturally into their places
under various obvious emblems. The OLIVE LEAVES
are Poems on Sacred, the CYPRESS LEAVES on Sorrowful subjects; the MYRTLE LEAVES are poetical recol-
lections of a more general character, interspersed with
word-sketches from nature; the IVY LEAVES, as in
Germany, are garlands for the interior of a happy

home; and these in turn, are succeeded by ORANGE BLOSSOMS, which are twined for inmate after inmate of that home, ere each departs. The MAY BLOSSOMS are dedicated to children, and are in some danger of being thought trivial by all beside.

Several of these poems have in past years found their way *singly* into many households, and have ministered solace, through the blessing of God, to the sick and the weary. That named "The Border Land" has been often printed separately, and has had, under the form of a fly-sheet, a very wide circulation in the chambers of suffering and death. This, with other pieces of like character (composing the OLIVE LEAVES), is now reprinted, with the hope that the whole may prove acceptable. Not one of them was originally written for publication. Not a leaf in the garland can lay claim to very high poetical merit. The author can only hope that if any part of it is fitted to give pleasure or comfort to those who choose to gather it, stern critics in rhythm and metre may forbear to rend it asunder.

DECEMBER, 1854.

CONTENTS.

OLIVE LEAVES.

vi

MYRTLE LEAVES.

CONTENTS.

IVY LEAVES.

ORANGE BLOSSOMS.

MAY BLOSSOMS.

CYPRESS LEAVES.

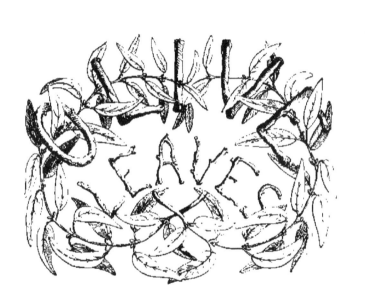

THE WANDERING HEART.

ALAS, for the wildly wandering heart,
   And its changing idol guests,
It has roam'd away to the world's far ends,
   At the vagrant wind's behests;
More fleet in its course than the flying dart,—
      Alas, for the wandering heart!

Go, bind it with memory's holiest spells,
   But it recks not things of old;
Go, chain it in gratitude's surest cells,
   With fairer fetters than gold;
Yet ever, oh ever, it will depart,—
      Alas, for the wandering heart!

Is it gone up to listen at heaven's gate,
   To Gabriel's lyre of praise?
To catch the deep chanting where seraphs wait,
   So framing its mortal lays?
Oh, no; for it loves from such lessons to part,—
      Alas, for the wandering heart!

2

It loves, on a worthless and treach'rous world
    To bestow its high desires,—
The lamp which it ought to have lighted in heaven,
    It kindles at idol fires;
Full seldom it turns to its guiding chart,—
     Alas, for the wandering heart!

It needs to be steep'd in the briny wave
    Of affliction's billowy sea,
And salt tears must water its way to the grave,
    Ere 'twill from these vanities flee;
It must ever be feeling the chastening smart,—
     Alas, for the wandering heart!

My Father! my Father! this heart would be thine!
    Restore from its wanderings;
Oh, visit and nourish thy wilderness vine,
    Although from the bitter springs:
Till the years of its pruning in time shall be o'er,
     And its shoots in eternity wander no more!

"RETURN THEE TO THY REST."

PSALM CXVI. 7.

RETURN, return thee to thine only rest,
　　Lone pilgrim of the wold!
　　Far erring from the fold—
By the dark night and risen storms distress'd;
List, weary lamb, the Shepherd's anxious voice,
And once again within his arms rejoice.

Return, return! thy fair white fleece is soil'd,
　　And by sharp briers rent—
　　Thy little strength is spent;
Yet He will pity thee, thou torn and spoil'd.
There, thou art cradled on his tender breast,
Now never more, sweet lamb, forsake that rest.

Return, return, my soul! be like this lamb.
　　Yet can it, can it be
　　That Thou should'st pardon me,
Thou injured Love! all ingrate as I am;
Once again, weary of earth's trifling things,
False as the desert's far and shining springs?

Return, return to thy forsaken Friend,
　　So long despised, forgot—
　　That should He " know thee not,"
The " wandering heart" his justice must defend:

Yet on, press on, towards the mercy-seat,
And if thou perish, perish at his feet.

Return, return, for He is near thee dwelling,
   And not into the air
   Need rise the sighs of prayer;
Into his ear thou'rt all thy sorrows telling;
Thou need'st not speak to Him through spaces wide,
For He is near thee, even at thy side.

" Him have I pierced "—oh! I come, I come;
   My heart is broken, Lord,
   It needs nor voice nor word;
One only look brought Peter back of yore;
How bitterly I weep, as then *he* wept!
Henceforth, oh, keep me, and I shall be kept.

A MEDITATION.

" And went backward, and not forward."—*Jer.* vii. 24.

EVEN so—like wand'ring Israel,
   Straying from the paths of peace,
Bound to the far land of promise,
   Through the barren wilderness,
Yet, unmindful of their home,
Content amongst the sands to roam.

Amongst the sands of earth, O Lord!
  The trifles of the day,
My soul hath linger'd long, nor pass'd
  Upon its onward way:
" Backward, and not forward" pressing,
Though the light of life possessing.

Earth hath snares for flesh and spirit,
  Suited to a wand'ring heart,
Satan numbs it to the power
  Even of the chast'ning smart:
And its own deceitful dealings!
Who can count its evil feelings?

Lord, thus tempted, and thus yielding
  Ever to idolatry,
Didst Thou, couldst thou bear with Israel?
  Wilt Thou, canst Thou bear with me?
Alas! though froward and perverse,
Did Israel ever tempt Thee thus?

Yet Thou leddest them home at last,
  By the fire, and by the cloud;
And me, by fiery trial prove,
  In the clouds of sorrow shroud,
If these I need,—ere I be driven
To seek a better rest in heaven.

A LESSON OF STILL.

"He leadeth me beside the still waters."—*Ps.* xxiii. 2.

" ' A LESSON of still'—what a very odd title!" It is so, kind reader; and if you do not happen to belong to the Society of Friends, who would understand it at once, we must introduce you to Miss Emily Horton, a quiet invalid, who, as she lies upon her sofa, has been thinking about it, and she shall explain it in your hearing to a gentle and pleasant friend, who is come with her work-bag to spend an hour by her side.

"And so, dear Emily, you sent me word that you had been taking ' a lesson of still.' If it will not tire you to talk, will you tell me what you mean?"

"I was thinking, my dear madam, of a young Quakeress I met at Sidmouth last year. She had three lovely children; and sometimes when I have been spending the day with her, she has called one of them to her knee, saying, ' Now, little Mary dear, let us have a lesson of still;' she would then take out her watch, and, for five or ten minutes, the child would seat itself in its small chair, and remain perfectly quiet. They were very early trained to this habit, and were remarkably happy and good children."

"Well, my love, and now for the application."

"I think that as their mother acted towards them, my heavenly Father is now acting towards me; and I wanted you, dear Mrs. Lardner, to come and help me to learn the lessons which He is meaning to teach me."

"Most willingly, if it is in my power, though you are

looking already to teaching which is better than mine. Was this young mother in the habit of presenting to the child's mind any food for thought at these times of ' still ?'"

" Occasionally she would whisper in its ear a text of Scripture, or a verse of a hymn, which she had previously impressed upon its recollection; but I believe that the habit was formed, as a foundation for the serenity and peace of demeanour which you know belongs to that denomination of Christians, and which it would be well for every child of God to cultivate in whatever division of the fold."

" And now, my dear, supposing yourself to be this child in God's hand, how were you employed when it pleased Him thus to say to you, ' Be still'? You have been laid aside for several weeks, to the sorrow of many a kind friend; indeed I have much sympathy to bear to you this morning, from those whom you are yet unable to see."

" I am sure I thank them for their sympathy; but if they knew how needful this stillness has been to me spiritually, they would rejoice in my affliction, rather than sorrow for it. You asked me what occupied me when I was taken ill? As far as action was concerned, I was at work in God's vineyard, and have been compelled to leave my work at a time when there seemed the most for me to do."

• " You do not speak this as a murmur, Emily!"

" No, my dear friend, I trust not *now;* for if this was my feeling at first, God has further humbled me, and shown me that He can well dispense with my little all of effort and energy. I have noticed that, with all your tenderness which abounds towards me, you have not once yourself expressed sorrow for my present disabilities, in common with my other friends."

" Because, my beloved, it is not my habit to express sorrow for the dispensations of a heavenly Father to his chil-

dren. I endeavour to watch against it. These dispensations
are exactly fitted to our need, and this is fitted to yours.
Whilst I would comfort you under your affliction, I desire
that *you* should look upon it as a mercy from Heaven, and
dive deeply into your own heart, to find out why it comes.
'Show me wherefore thou contendest with me!' My own
soul has so often found the greenest pasture after the falling
of the dark cloud, that I dare not wish for my best friends,
that they should never dwell beneath its shadow."

"That is the voice of one who has felt, as I am feeling now,
the blessings of the brook Cherith. I have been reading that
good book of Dr. Krummacher's, 'Elijah the Tishbite.' In
speaking of situations where we must be alone with God, he
says, 'By these we are shut in with Elijah, by the brook
Cherith. But such seclusion, how blissful and salutary may it
become! Numberless Christians have been constrained to declare that it was in their lonely sick chamber that they entered
really into their own hearts, and ascertained their true spiritual state. The leaven of the pharisees was then put away
from them, and worship was no longer paid to an imaginary
Saviour. They began to long in earnest for close communion
with Him; and the wrestling prayer of Jacob, lasting until
day-break, which they had only talked of before, now became
a matter of reality and experience, an event in their own personal history; and a hundred other things, pertaining to
inward religion, which they had only in imagination appro-
priated hitherto, were then individually realized. Therefore,
be of good cheer, ye that dwell by the brook Cherith.'"

"I am glad such a book has found its way to you just
now. Books are quiet friends; and we should take care of
their character at all times, but especially in sickness. A
light, trifling volume then, will fritter away the sound of the
still small voice of God; and in that case, why are we here

alone? But you must not read much at present. Remember,
it is 'a lesson of still' to body and mind. I hear your physician prescribes two moral medicines, patience and repose,
and says to you, 'Be content to lie fallow a little longer.' Is
this difficult, my child?"

"Very difficult, but I find it is necessary. The character
of my disorder is lingering and relapsing; I have gone back
again several times after getting forward too soon, and rise
from each attack with added weakness. I am told I should
save my strength as it returns, and not use it again directly:
but this is a new lesson to one of active habits; and it is, as
you say, 'difficult.'"

"I dare say it was difficult to the little rosy child in the
small chair at first; but the principles which were enough for
her, will suffice for you—Love and obedience to Him 'who
maketh thee to lie down in green pastures—who leadeth thee
beside the still waters; for so He restoreth thy soul.' I trust
He will be pleased ere long to restore bodily health likewise.
I should like to give you a hint or two on this head."

"You have long been my Mentor both for body and mind.
I should like to know what the hint would be."

"I have long studied you, Emily: you are by nature the
ardent and energetic creature of extremes. It has pleased
God in his wisdom to surround you with friends, and to place
you under a dispensation which checks this tendency; otherwise you would have been less useful in the world than you
are now. He has shed his grace abroad in your heart, and
disposed you to consecrate all your energies and powers to
his service; but you are still the creature of extremes: your
enthusiasm does great things in itself, and by its example,
and they are things of the right kind—they tell upon the
conversion of sinners to Christ; but you do too much at once,
and this occasions you to work rather fitfully than steadily:

we hear of you as accomplishing wonders in one month, but the next finds you laid aside, and able to do nothing."

" Yes, it is true, and I know it. I often wonder that any one depends upon me to direct or influence them at all, for I am so often breaking my engagements, through illness; but how is this to be helped?"

" *By self-regulation.* Your present illness has been coming on for some time,—extremes are its cause. I notice that sorrow and joy have almost an equal effect upon you: you sink after each, into a state of debility. This is the result of that delicately strung nervous system, which often appertains to intellectual persons, and which it should be their aim to invigorate, rather than to task to its utmost power. You are one of those who should never go out of your way to seek excitement: enough of it, as much as you can bear, is sure to come to you in daily and common life. I have not to warn you against the dissipations of the world, you have no taste for them; but the society of few and chosen friends, and of the right kind too, is often not less injurious to you, phy-sically: you enjoy it intensely, more perhaps than most others do, and so you pay for the added pleasure with the superadded pain."

" But you would not have me less employed in the service of God, my dear Mrs. Lardner? My heart burns for the salva-tion of the world. I feel it to be the chief end of life to add a mite of effort into this treasury. Are not souls now perish-ing for lack of knowledge? I lie here, uselessly, and this makes me weep; but, no, it is ' the lesson of still.' "

" And to learn it, dearest, is your duty. There are hun-dreds, on the contrary, to whom it might be said, ' Arise, go work in the vineyard.' Shake off the selfishness of ease— and behold the field of the world. You will however be more fitted to arouse these slumberers, when you have learned this

' lesson of still.' You will have passed through the furnace, and, I trust, will come forth as gold: your efforts will not be made so much in your own strength, but Christ will work in you to ' the pulling down of strong holds.' Your present debility is the medicine given by your heavenly Physician. Do not be impatient for its removal—' the cup which my Father hath given me, shall I not drink it?' Avoid anxiety, leave all to God. Do not think that while *you* are standing still, all that depends upon you is doing the same—this retards recovery: and when health and strength do return, one word more about the way to keep them—regular habits, simple and sufficient diet, and early hours. More jealously than ever watch over your seasons of meditation and prayer. The nearer, day by day, you keep to the foot of the cross, and the more you dwell upon your Saviour's character—the less unduly excited you will be with aught ' that is of the earth, earthy,' whether pleasurably or painfully. There are few circumstances in life about which it is worth while to be much excited; and so we think, the nearer we come to the journey's end. But you have been writing a little, I see. May I read these lines? I suppose it would be very hard to deny you a visit from the Muses sometimes, as you lie here alone."

" Oh! I have nothing to do with those titled ladies of ancient fable. Mine are simple endeavours to express and embody some feelings now and then, which I wish to recollect, and which would otherwise be forgotten; these few lines are the history of half-an-hour this morning. They are part of an Apology for Romance, addressed to Reason, who despises her:—

> ' More lofty and severe art Thou.
> But oft when sickness pales the brow
> She comes to cheer the silent calm
> That follows suffering's keen alarm;

The voice of friendship then might tire,
But her's, more softly can inspire
The soul upon itself to muse,
And from the stores of memory choose
(Where radiant pictures treasured lie,
Treasured when health and hope were high,)
Some sun-set glow—some morning gray—
Some mountain lone—some woodland way,
Which oft shall lull relapsing pain
Till freedom is our own again.'"

"Yes, I think this is permissible pleasure, and happy the mind which has these stores, and the power of communicating them to others. I will leave you now, with one further wish—that this time of seclusion and repose for the body may be a season of great progress in your spiritual pilgrimage. It is in seasons like these that we detect a worm at the root of the motive of many a fair and lovely action, and get clear views of the ground that is yet to be possessed. I have brought you this short extract from a sermon on 'Eminent Piety essential to Eminent Usefulness :'*—'We may, like the disciples, have been converted from darkness unto light, but we may yet want that elevation of Christian character which, for its importance, may be regarded as *a second conversion*, and which is essential to advanced enjoyment and extensive usefulness; we then must become as 'little children,' nothing in our own esteem, separated from the luxuries and carnal indulgences of life—without covetousness; without ambition, resting on the resources of superior wisdom and power; and this must take place in us before we can greatly contribute to the coming triumphs of Christianity in the world.' This is a passage which I am sure you will delight to study and to realize. Farewell."

* By Dr. Andrew Reed.

THE BORDER LAND.

I HAVE been to a land, a Border Land,
   Where was but a strange dim light;
Where shadows and dreams, in a spectral band,
   Seem'd real to the aching sight.
I scarcely bethought me how there I came,
   Or if thence I should pass again;
Its morning and night were mark'd by the flight,
   Or coming, of woe and pain.

But I saw from this land, this Border Land,
   With its mountain ridges hoar,
That they look'd across to a wondrous strand,
   A bright and unearthly shore.
Then I turn'd me to Him, " *the Crucified*,"
   In most humble faith and prayer,
Who had ransom'd with blood my sinful soul;
   For I thought He would call me there.

Yet, nay: for awhile in the Border Land
   He bade me in patience stay,
And gather rich fruits, with a trembling hand,
   Whilst He chased its glooms away.
He had led me amid those shadows dim,
   And shown that bright world so near,
To teach me that earnest trust in Him
   Is " the one thing needful" here.

And so from the land, yes, the Border Land,
   I 've turn'd me to earth once more;
But earth and its works were all trifles, scann'd
   By the light of that radiant shore.
And, oh! should they ever possess me again
   Too deeply, in heart and hand,
I must think how empty they seem'd, and vain,
   From the heights of the Border Land.

The Border Land had depths and vales,
   Where sorrow for sin was known ;
Where small seem'd great, as weigh'd in scales,
   Held by God's hand alone.
'Twas a land where earthly pride was naught,
   Where the poor were brought to mind,
With their scanty bed, their fireless cot,
   And their bread so hard to find.

But little I heard in the Border Land
   Of the din that pass'd below;
For the once loud voices of human life
   To the deafen'd ear were low.
I was deaf to the clang of its trumpet call,
   And alike to its gibe or its sneer ;
Its riches were dust, and the loss of all
   Would then scarce have cost a tear.

I met with a Friend in this Border Land,
   Whose teachings can come with power
To the blinded eye and the deafen'd ear,
   In affliction's loneliest hour.

And " times of refreshing " to the soul,
   In its languor, oft He brings,
Preparing it then to meditate
   On high and glorious things.

Oh! Holy Ghost! too often grieved,
   In my health and earthly haste,
How I bless those slow and silent hours
   Which appear'd to run to waste!
I would not *but* have pass'd those " depths,"
   And such full communion known,
As there can be held in the Border Land,
   With Thee, and with Thee alone.

Thou takest there " of the things of Christ,"
   A past and a future page,
And Thou pourest on each divinest light,
   At steps of our pilgrimage,
Diverse—as every soul can bear.
   Of such light, in times of old,
King David, when brought to the Border Land,
   Oft sang to his harp of gold.

And I went to this land, this Border Land,
   Sweetest charities to prove;
For the hours betwixt life and death demand
   Deepest springs and founts of love.
Yet not mother's love, though strong and dear,
   Hath power to heal or save,
If the time be come, and the call be clear,
   To the coffin and the grave.

I have been to a land, a Border Land!
  May oblivion never roll,
O'er the mighty lessons which there and then,
  Have been graven on my soul!
I have trodden a path I did not know,
  Safe in my Saviour's hand:
I can trust Him for all the future, now
  I have been to the Border Land.

1847.

"A BROKEN CISTERN ALL THE WHILE."

A MEDITATION.

DURING THE ABSENCE OF FRIENDS AT CONISTON.

WHY is it, when a sunny gleam of light,
A pleasant dole from heaven's treasury bright,
  Of all things beautiful and good that seem,
Falls transient on my daily even way,
'Tis scarcely own'd and blest, before I say,
  " Behold the *shadow* close upon the gleam"?

'Tis true that joy is ever ecstasy;
Is really more than simple joy to me:
  It comes not oft, as gladness to the gay;

Secret and rarely felt, it mostly lies
In old associate, hidden, sympathies,
   Deep and intense, that wake not every day.

In early youth—in days when hope was high,
A somewhat was discern'd in Friendship's eye
   And in fair Nature's face, sublime or soft,
That brought such exquisite delight, it vied
With all the syren Hope had prophesied;
   Then, on such joy did suffering follow oft.

And *now*, when to a mind of deeper tone,
And richer memories—such joys would come,
   Why is it that Denial cold and stern
Is Hope's perpetual handmaid? why, oh why?
My heart, in patience quell that rising sigh;
   And in retirement, holier lesson learn.

There is a world beyond this world of shows,
The thought whereon God wills thee to repose:
   Thereto He points thee in thy lonely hours.
Communings here with kindred souls denied,
Shall, in that " world to come," be satisfied.
   Joy dwelleth there,—not on this earth of ours.

Thou shalt *not* dress a Paradise below;
And couldst thou all Earth's loftiest converse know,
   Abiding with its purest and its best:
And if its fairest scenery could combine
To prison and suffice this soul of thine,
   God bids it forth, on a more glorious quest.

Him thou must seek! to Him thy being tend!
He is thy " Lord," thy " Life," thy " Joy," thy " Friend;"
   Thy spirit striveth for a nobler birth.
If aught from Him would lure thee to depart,
Then must it be withheld, thou " wandering heart;"
   Thine home is not upon the doomed earth.

For this He cleareth thee a space of rest,
Full oft from many cares, to be a guest
   Alone with Him : a gift of grace unsought.
When thou shalt enter it without repining,
Experience in peace his sun's clear shining,
   And know no will but his, the end is wrought.

Then, be it so, that others round me smile,
And I, " A BROKEN CISTERN, ALL THE WHILE ;"
   Yes, be it so, if such the lot for me.
Better than, fill'd with Earth's delights, to miss
The o'erflowings of God's love in hours like this,
   Which I may treasure in Eternity.

    High Close, 1849.

"WHOM THE LORD LOVETH HE CHASTENETH."

HEBREWS XII. 6.

A PSALM FOR A SICK ROOM.

AGAIN I feel—O God—
Stripes of thy bitter rod :
All suddenly they come, and sharp the pain :
    Almighty—Wilt Thou deign
To give account to me or reason why?
    Nay : Thou dost but reply,
" I CHASTEN WHOM I LOVE ":
Balm for thy bitter stripes, all else above.

    Therefore, while chain'd and bound
    With links of suffering round,
I wait in patience on this weary bed ;
    I know, Lord, Thou hast said,
That thou wilt ne'er allot *one* woe or care
    More than thy child can bear.
" I CHASTEN WHOM I LOVE :"
In that sweet thought is balm, all else above.

    'Tis good for thee, my heart,
    Thus to be set apart

Against thy will, from all thy works and ways.
God also will have praise
From helplessness, so thou faint not, nor tire.
What more canst thou desire?
" I CHASTEN WHOM I LOVE:"
Feed on that thought! 'tis balm, all else above.

I chasten them, to wean
From each enchanting scene,
The children of a kingdom yet to come:
Fair stones, to be brought home,
All chisell'd as they needed, at my will;
Each one its place to fill
In the temple of my love—
The radiant New Jerusalem above.

" I CHASTEN WHOM I LOVE."
I could not teach or move
Man's spirit thus, amid life's whirling shows:
But I can give repose
In long, lone, wakeful nights, to the poor heart,
With which it ne'er shall part;
And bid each promise beam
Out in the darkness, with most lustrous gleam.

Rejoice, my chasten'd ones,
My daughters and my sons
Walk softly in the way ye have been led.
By tribulation dead
Should *ye* be to earth's pomp and lust of gain,
And all its warfare vain;

Check'd every low desire,
Have ye not pass'd through the Refiner's fire?

Rejoice, my chasten'd ones!
How were ye proved "Sons"
Unless in following your Exalted Head,
Who, bruised, faint, and dead,
Refused not to brave the inner gloom
Of the drear tomb?
Endure in peace your pain,
For "those who suffer with Him, also reign."

Jesus! our risen Lord!
Who dost to us afford
Thy promised gift, the Comforter, below,
How should we ever know
His rich, peculiar teaching of the word,
Did suffering not accord
The soften'd heart and calm,
On which He may bestow his healing balm?

Yes, chasten'd ones, rejoice!
Afflictions, not *your* choice,
Are yet God's ministers most wisely sent,
And in His mercy lent,
That tears for secret sin may freely flow,
And self and pride lie low.
" I CHASTEN WHOM I LOVE:"
Feed on that thought! 'tis balm, all else above.

1850.

"BEAR YE ONE ANOTHER'S BURDENS."

" Bear ye one another's burdens, and so fulfil the law of Christ."–*Gal.* vi. 2.
" Every man shall bear his own burden."–*Gal.* vi. 5.

THIS precept, seeming to oppose the assertion, is found not far from it, in the letter of the apostle Paul to the churches of Galatia; but it appears from the context, that while the same word " burden" is used in each verse, in the *precept* it relates to affliction and weight of trouble, and in the *assertion* it refers to individual responsibility, and concerns burdens which our fellow-creatures have no power to relieve. Both precept and assertion are worthy of patient thought; and, taking them in their order, we will endeavour to enforce them.

" Bear ye one another's burdens" is a well-understood precept; for we have all burdens, small or great,—some crook in the lot, some thorn in the flesh; and we all like sympathy under their pressure. How cold and weary is a life without sympathy! If there be a man who, by his position, is deprived—or who, by his temper, has deprived himself of a friend, with whom to share his troubles, he is a miserable creature, at the close of the loftiest career. If we have ever watched the course of a proud and independent mind, we shall have seen that it is not happy, with all its greatness, unless it finds fellowship with some one of its kind; not so much in intellectual community, as in loving and being loved again. This is the final necessity of human nature. God made it so in its first estate of innocence, and he has left it so, even in its present guilt and degradation by sin. We need

friends with whom to dwell upon the lights of life, and these
are readily found to rejoice when we rejoice. We draw yet
more closely to them amidst its shadows, that they may weep
with us when we weep; and if they then become fewer, they
are dearer. Afflictions show us our friends, as prosperity
finds us our flatterers.

Now, it is not, perhaps, enough remembered, that the sympathy we desire to receive, we must be found willing to bestow. We must do and feel unto others as we would that
they should do and feel unto us; and if we are ready to bear
the burdens of our friends—to identify ourselves cordially
with their anxieties, difficulties, sufferings, losses, and crosses,
we shall find our own burdens lifted from our shoulders, as
far as may be, in the hour of need.

It strikes us, as the sum of our experience, that every man
receives in this way about as much as he really deserves.
The selfish person claims more than he deserves—demands to
receive that which he has never accorded to others; and
always complains, in most bitter terms, of want of sympathy,
and of the world's ingratitude.

When, therefore, we feel ourselves disposed to murmur at
a lack of fellowship, let us look around us, and endeavour to
exhibit more of it towards others. If we complain, and with
some reason, that a person whom we might expect to assist
us in bearing our burdens, looks coldly upon us, let us first
examine if he has any burdens to bear, and if we have sought
to bear them. Let us watch whether we have been willing
to approve his plans, to pass leniently over his failures, to
congratulate him on his successes, and to view all that he
does in a favourable light; for this is what we like to be done
to us, and such sympathy is tolerably sure to meet with its
return.

It is a duty in those who have to bear the burden of life

together, in husband and wife especially, and, indeed, in all
the other near relations of society, to bear each other's burdens of a minor kind, as well as those of greater magnitude.
And this also is much neglected. If there be found among
the members of our circle some of sickly body and weak
mind, or of fretful and complaining temper, we must bear
with them; and this does not mean that we should coldly
tolerate them, but that we should soothe and conceal their
infirmities as much as may be; yet how often do we act as if
deformity of temper and deficiency of sense had absolved us
from all tender consideration, and thereby increase, rather
than bear, the burden of the sufferers. If we love persons
truly, we shall, of course, endeavour rather to cover than
expose their weak points, and not talk of the burdens we
have to bear on their account. Our Redeemer sees these
burdens, and notes our behaviour under them; He measures
out to us our every-day weight of small crosses, and observes
whether, through self-denial and crucifixion of the flesh with
its affections and lusts, we are being led towards the crown
which He has prepared for those who love Him—who take up
their cross and follow Him. Have we not all somewhat to
confess in this particular?

But it is also written, "Every man shall bear his own burden"—shall endure the weight of his own responsibility.
No one mortal being can answer for another at the bar of
God; and if we have not in this life found the burden of sin
roll off at the foot of the cross, as in Bunyan's beautiful alle-
gory—if our Saviour has not borne the weight of the curse
for us, heavy will be the burden which must crush us into
hell. If, however, we have sought and found this Saviour,
and if we are so happy as to possess in our relative earthly
connexions, all that can be expected of kindly sympathy, still
each heart knoweth its own bitterness; and there is some

burden, secret, if not visible, that we must separately bear.
The husband cannot bear it for the wife, nor the wife for the
husband. The tender mother, great as is her faculty of sympathy, cannot bear it for the child; and she feels this when
she sees her little one tortured by personal pain, beyond her
power of relief. Some have much more strength than others
to strive against the outward manifestations of these personal burdens. The children of this world have their burdens—their losses, crosses, and cares, under which many of
them are irritated to exasperation and self-destruction; whilst
those of a more placid temperament often bear them with a
stoicism which astonishes us. When bereaved, ill, and dis-
appointed in their dearest schemes, their demeanour will often
read a lesson to the fretful and irritable Christian, (strange
anomaly in terms!) who ought to know, and does know, that
all things are working together for his good; and thus the
men of this world are said to be " wiser in their generation
than the children of light." They are taught that it is un-
manly to be disturbed about trifles—undignified to confess
that they have any burden to bear; and while they often
maintain a hollow repose, and mere outside show of peace,
they shame, by comparison, those who really possess " a friend
that sticketh closer than a brother,"—one who, when the heart
knoweth its own bitterness, knoweth even the heart also, and
can either " remove the shoulder from the burden," (Psa.
lxxxi. 6,) or ease its pressure with the mighty words, " My
grace is sufficient for thee: for my strength is made perfect
in weakness." (2 Cor. xii. 9.) Yes, every man must bear his
own burden, till he has faith to cast it upon the Lord, knowing that He will sustain it.

In this life the written communication of thoughts and
facts takes up so much time and power, that when the friends
who were brought up by our side become distant, if we and

they are much occupied, they lose communion with our daily
identity, and we with theirs. Each one of us " bears his own
burden," and each one is so filled with his own affairs (for
our minds are naturally self-occupied), that when the long-
parted meet again, from different spheres, neither one cares
to communicate or to hear, as in olden time, the peculiar
troubles of the other. There are, of course, exceptions to
this statement; but we think that the prevalence of its truth
makes up the heartlessness of society. People in general are
far more interested in speaking of their own affairs, than in
listening to those of others. Every man bears his own burden; and it is the few who bear others' burdens, and in so
doing, forget their own.

But though unto every one born into the world, is appointed his share of the burden of life, there are burdens which we take to ourselves when we need not do so,
which Satan places as temptations in our path, to see if
we will pick them up, and load ourselves with them, to our
hindrance in the heavenward way. The yoke of Christ is
easy, and his burden is light; but we often get weary and
heavy laden with burdens which we have no occasion to
court. For instance, we go out of a straightforward course
of duty to secure that which we think will be an advantage,
or to avert what seems to us an impending loss, and we attain
our end, being determined to do so; and we afterwards find
that we had been wiser had we suffered the event to pass as
it would have done, without our care; and that God would
have judged better for us in the addition or subtraction, had
we permitted his guidance.

The things which are accomplished for us, without our
own intervention, are mostly the right things, and done in the
right time ; and those which we are resolved to have and to
do for ourselves, without looking to providential guidance,

prove, after all, our burdens; under the weight of which we must reflect that they were taken up of our own accord, and whose pressure we have to feel perhaps for a life-time.

Some take unto themselves the burden of riches, and so " fall into temptation and a snare." They rise early and sit up late, and eat the bread of carefulness; but it is only to obtain the gold that perisheth, and sometimes by unlawful means ;—whether by such trade as ruins the souls of others, or by a tissue of small secret dishonesties in word and deed, to which they yielded first in hours of temptation; sins of committal or of omission, never perhaps known to a fellow-creature, never forgotten by themselves and the recording angel; and which must one day, if pardon through the blood of Christ prevent not,

> " Be all exposed before the sun
> While men and angels hear."

Confession, contrition, and restitution are necessary to the falling off of this burden.

Those who launch out in trade and speculation upon ficti-tious capital, thereby making to themselves an excess of busi-ness, pick up a burden which they need not have done; and find it a great spiritual hindrance, whether it tend to cum-brous riches, or to loss and poverty. For riches themselves, when attained, are often a burden: they bring with them the supposed necessity of doing as others do; and presently in their train come the fatigue and anxiety of a large establish-ment, which many complain of and groan under, who yet would be far from willing to renounce their burden, and descend to a life without pomp or show. The taking of this burden upon us mostly depends upon ourselves, as does the converse,—the burden of poverty, whether brought on by vice, by carelessness, by imprudence, or by want of foresight. How bitterly must each of these be afterwards regretted! There is a melancholy history in the words, " He brought himself to poverty"; and the sufferer in such circumstances must recall its details more bitterly than one who can trace his losses clearly and truly to the misconduct of others.

The same must be said of unchristian marriages : " Be ye not unequally yoked together with unbelievers," is the decided command ; and if the children of God are tempted to transgress it, they take a burden to themselves that is sure to gall them somewhere, and constantly to prove a hindrance in their way to heaven. So of reading bad or doubtful books : ideas may, by our own act, be introduced into our minds, which may make our days and nights restless, and destroy the peace of our consciences. They are not less seductive than bad companions, and should be resolutely put from us, as we would avoid the plague. Let us avoid taking to ourselves such burdens for the amusement of the hour,—for it is hard to disinfect the memory, when once tainted with evil ; and " blessed are the pure in heart : for they shall see God."

Every parent shall bear his own burden as children grow up, who does not, while young, hold them under restraint from that which is bad, and guide them towards that which is good. The seed-time being lost, where is the harvest ?

In his early days, in his thoughtless youth, what an age of repentance, what a burden for life, has many a young man brought upon himself, by half an hour of mischievous frolic ! The loss of limb or sense, perhaps, is caused by him, or he inflicts irreparable injury on the mind or body of his companion.

We should be concerned not to bring our burdens on ourselves, by allowing small offences and jealousies to rankle in our minds, and there to grow into greater importance than they deserve. Inoccupancy is a fruitful ground, on which this sin may grow. " A soft answer turneth away wrath"; but the reciprocation or repetition to another of the cross look, and hard word, adds to our own burden, if we have any such to bear; neither do we "suffer with Christ," unless, when reviled, we revile not again.

It is of no use to seek for perfect communion of feeling in this world: "Every man shall bear his own burden"; and it is a pity to get offended with people because they do not identify themselves with our interests and concerns as much as we may expect. Friends change, and die; and those are the most secure of happiness who depend upon God and themselves for it. And then, however transplanted and however isolated, they are not habitually sighing for the want of sympathy; and are the more thankful when it occasionally crosses them.

To conclude with the wise advice of Fenelon:—" Never allow yourself to be irritated, and so take up a burden from the discourse of your fellow-creatures. Let them talk, and do you try to do the will of God. As to that of man, you will never accomplish doing it; it is not even worth the trouble of trying. A little silence, peace, and union with God ought easily to console you for anything that men may unjustly say. We ought to love them without depending on their friendship; they abandon and they return to us. Let them go and come; they resemble the feather which the wind carries away. Look to God alone in them. He alone comforts or afflicts us by their instrumentality, according as our need is."

Finally: it is well for every one to bear his own burden patiently and cheerfully, for he might probably be less able to bear either the good, or the ill allotted to another person ;

and it is not always wise to pray for the removal of our burdens, but always for their sanctification. May they urge us
daily towards a throne of grace, and quicken our progress
towards that world where—

> " From the burden of the flesh,
>   And from care and fear released,
>   All the wicked cease from troubling,
>   And the weary are at rest."

1851.

BEAR IT.

"Charity beareth all things."—1 *Cor.* xv. 7.

FOLLOWER of the lowly Lamb,
    Hast thou ceased to watch and pray?
O'er what neighbour's faults and sins
    Hast thou cast the veil to-day?
If thou answ'rest scorn with scorn,
    Adding to the heap of ill,
Art thou of the Spirit born?
    Workest thou the Father's will?

Bear it—yes, in silence bear it,
    Bitter howsoe'er it be ;
Not a human ear must share it,
    Known alone to God and Thee:

Secret griefs shall train thy soul
   Into finer sympathies
With Him who makes the wounded whole;
   *And calls all their sorrows—*His*.

Bear it—Christ hath borne before thee
   All that hate and malice flung;
Healing balm He can shed o'er thee,
   For the arrows of the tongue.
Only bear it—hush complaint—
   Nor to men thy cross betray:
Nor revile again, nor faint;
   Follow on—thy Master's way.

Bear it—When *He*, the world's high Lord,
   Came to his thankless own;
His perfect goodness was abhorr'd,
   Despised, and all unknown.
And who art *thou*—to speak of wrong,
   Or to weep for want of love,
If *He* the scorners sat among,
   Heaven's pure, incarnate Dove?

Follower of the lowly Lamb,
   Never cease to watch and pray;
Hide thy wounds from all but Jesus,
   Prayer can smooth the roughest way!
And such endurance in thee wrought,
   Or thy cross shall lifted be;
Or thou wouldst not with it part,
   So tenderly 'tis borne for thee.

Bear it—He but bids thee bear
  Whate'er thy spirit needs ;
Till, like unto a garden fair,
  All weeded of its weeds,
It yield him fruits and spices sweet,
  Press'd out by his own hand ;
And thou, by slow degrees made meet,
  Shalt reach the Promised Land.

1849.

OPPORTUNITIES.

" All that thou mightest have been!
All that thou mightest have done!"

MARK that long dark line of shadows,
  Stretching far into the past:
Every day it seems to lengthen :
  Whither does it tend at last?
Each one added to the hosts
  From the present moment flies:
These are Time's forgotten ghosts,
  Fleeted opportunities.

Characters of light or darkness—
  Gabriel's pen from each requires:
God records, if man forgets them ;
  Numbers each as each expires ;

And the awful spectres all
  At the day of doom will rise,
Witnesses at Heaven's call—
  Fleeted opportunities.

Buried powers of good unmeasured,
  Hardly present did ye seem ;
Yet I thought I should have treasured,
  When ye vanish'd like a dream.
Crushing now my sinful soul,
  All your weight upon it lies ;
Jesu's blood must o'er ye roll,
  Fleeted opportunities.

Oh, my soul! no further lengthen
  Wilfully this ghostly train ;
Rise, and seek for grace to strengthen,
  Where 'twas never sought in vain.
Lost, this hour but adds another
  To those solemn witnesses :
Every living soul's thy brother,—
  Mark thine opportunities.

1845.

"I WILL NOT GO OUT FREE."

" And if the servant shall say, I love my master. I will not go out free,
then he shall serve him for ever."—*Exod.* xxi. 5.

" And Simon Peter answered Him, Lord, to whom shall we go? Thou
hast the words of eternal life."—*John* vi. 68.

Go free? my glorious Master,
   Forsake Thee for the world?
Ah, whither should I go? and where
   Mine exiled soul be hurl'd?
What is there in the changing earth
   To be preferr'd to Thee?
No; I love Thee, oh, my Master!
   I would not go out free.

Its gauds and its trifle treasures?—
   They shall be burnt with fire;
Its glories and its pleasures?—
   How wearily they tire!
Its loudly vaunted liberty
   Were slavery to me.
No; I love Thee, oh, my Master!
   I would not go out free.

Free from the ties of tenderness,
   And mercy undefiled;
Of Him who died, that I might be
   Not a bond-slave, but a child?

Henceforth, his light and easy yoke
  My willing choice shall be.
No; I love Thee, oh, my Master!
  And I will not go out free.

How rich thy saving grace!
  Less on my hold of Thee
Depends my hope of heaven at last
  Than on Thine hold of me.
Back to the weary wilderness
  Permit me not to flee.
I love Thee, oh, my Master!
  And I will not go out free.

1831.

"THE NAME WHICH IS ABOVE EVERY NAME."

PHILIPPIANS II. 9.

THERE is a name, so deeply traced
  On hearts that once were stone,
Though all beside were thence erased,
  That name would stand alone:—
The Saviour's name.—Believer! say,
How has it deepen'd, day by day?

In this low world whilst I abide,
  My heart is train'd for heaven:

Afflicted, scourged, and purified
　From sin's corroding leaven.
The end of all events the same,—
The deeper here to grave his name.

When first its flinty surface knew
The Spirit's softening power;
Beside this name stood others too,
　The idols of the hour.
But God hath pass'd it thro' the fire,
For earthly love and vain desire.

All other names the fire has tried,
　And worn their trace away;
This one the burning can abide,
　Clear in its fiercest ray:
And now it ne'er effaced can be,
So oft, my Lord, I've fled to Thee.

And yet, whene'er a beam divine
　Lights up my evil heart,
I ask me if indeed 'tis thine,
　Or if it acts a part?
So dark its thoughts, so vain its dreams,
So far it is from what it seems.

Oh, be that heart at last subdued
　To all thine holy will;
To meekness every day renew'd,
　Albeit by suffering still;
Thy name above all names should be,
Show forth thy glorious name in me!

1837.

QUIES.

THE night hath rest! its worth the weary know;
Balm doth its shades on tired limbs bestow:
    Sleep, gentle handmaid, waits
    At the still entrance-gates,
Soft lulling anxious thought and aching woe.

The grave hath rest! night of life's weary day,
The shroud's calm sleep for the once suffering clay,
    Till God shall raise afresh
    The garment of the flesh,—
The dust laid up in dust for heaven's array.

Sabbaths have rest! when the soul shakes her wings,
In Zion's courts, awhile from meaner things;
    Forgets her week-day care,
    Or learns its weight to bear,
While dews of heaven around the Spirit flings.

And heaven hath rest—the Sabbath of the sky!
No weary feet shall walk the world on high;
    No tear of trouble falls
    Within those jasper walls.
To gain this rest for me did Jesus die.

1833.

ANXIETY.

"He careth for you."—1 *Pet.* v. 7.

HERE let me rest,
And lay my thousand hopes and fears
   To sleep upon his breast.
      Away with tears.
The good of my desire He gives;
That, even in denial, lives.

      Here let me rest:
He can bestow it, if He please;
   I am his child confess'd;
      My need He sees,
And says that nought exceeds his love,
In earth below, or heaven above.

      Here let me rest.
If He withhold the precious boon,
   His wisdom chooseth best;
      In heaven's high noon,
I may discern that bliss attain'd,
In virtue of this prayer disdain'd.

Here let me rest,
Till this deep anxiousness depart,
  This yearning of the breast,
    And aching smart ;
Till faith shall light the sadden'd way,
And meekness bless a Father's " nay."

Here let me rest:
What, though the path of life no more
  In rainbow tints be drest,
    Bright as of yore!
Why mourns my soul the loosen'd ties
That bound it from the upper skies?

Here let me rest
In lowly love of Christ my Lord,
  Broken in spirit, rest
    On his rich word :
On Him rely, in Him abide ;
Portion nor treasure seek beside.

1835.

THE NEW DESIRE.

A FRAGMENT.

Oh God! my God! no longer I entreat,
  Nor sue as I have sued in times of yore,
That from eternal fulness thou shouldst mete
  Into my cup, some earthly blessing more.
All things lie treasured in thy bounteous store.
  Nor lower source I seek, than source divine.
Thou hast no less to give than heretofore;
  But now a new desire, oh, Lord! is mine:
It is—*to lose desire*, and know no will but THINE.

1836.

"HE WILL REST IN HIS LOVE."

ZEPHANIAH III. 17.

HIS LOVE—my thoughts come turn away
  From all less pure and holy things;
Dwell, by the Spirit's help, and stay,
Beneath this beam of heavenly day;
  Oh, wand'rers! fold your wings.

HIS LOVE—my heart, thou oft hast tried
  In earthly friends to place thy trust.
Do not earth's dearest links divide ;
And canst thou e'er be satisfied
With creatures—earth and dust ?

HIS LOVE—sweet refuge from despair,
  Forsaken e'en, upbraideth not ;
'Tis thine, my soul ; and canst thou e'er
Forget its depth, or slight its care,
  Or crave another lot?

HIS LOVE—that knows no change of mood,
  But rests, where it designs to save,
Till every sin it hath subdued,
And every rebel thought renew'd,
  Attends us to the grave.

'Tis shed our sinful hearts among,
  And fills beside all heaven above.
To tell it, mocks an angel's tongue :
By man redeem'd, it must be sung.
  All heaven is this—HIS LOVE.

1836.

"AND HIS SERVANTS SHALL SERVE HIM."

REVELATION XXII. 3.

IN heaven his servants serve Him!
  We shall find no idols there,
No allurements of temptation,
  And no need for fear and prayer.
There every thought is dwelling on
  The Redeemer's dying love ;
And harps of gold e'er hymn the praise
  Of the Lord, all praise above.

There where his holy will is done,
  And his wrath for ever stay'd,
HE dwells,—to whose purer brightness
  E'en the light of heaven is shade.
And through those courts the perfect just,
  And the sinless angels roam,
Rejoicing as their Saviour leads
  Every lost and saved one home.

And blight is in that clime unknown ;
  No night is there, nor pain,
No poison'd arrow e'er shall reach
  Those ransom'd ones again.

And their own evil hearts, refined,
　No worship of self shall know ;
The " dross," and " chaff," all left behind,
　Of the earthly mind below.

There no more hindrance of the flesh,
　Nor aught from the weary brain ;
The uptendings of the spirit
　In God's kingdom shall restrain.
In heaven his servants serve him,
　And no failing comes between
The service that they render Him,
　And the service that they mean.

In heaven his servants serve Him ;
　We shall find no idols there ;
No allurements of temptation,
　And no need for fear and prayer.
There every thought is dwelling on
　The Redeemer's dying love ;
And harps of gold e'er breathe the praise
　Of the Lord, all praise above.

1854.

"THE LONE STILL ROOM."

Know'st thou the time when torturing pain,
 Yielding at last to healing skill,
Doth yet from fear'd return constrain
 The sufferer to seclusion still ?
The lone, still room, the shaded light,
Excluding all of warm or bright.

Oh, dweller in that lone still room !
 Thou and thy God are there alone.
What hast thou 'mid its favouring gloom
 In silent penitence to own ?
For He, thy true confessor, knows
Thy need of this enforced repose.

The good Physician of the soul,
 Bathes thee in Gilead's priceless balm :
He woundeth, and He maketh whole,—
 His is the cure, and his the calm.
" He leads thee in his own right way :"
Lie still and love, and hope, and pray.

1850.

THE CHRISTIAN TO HIS SOUL,

IN THE HOUR OF DEPARTURE.

I HAVE done with earth—the hour is nigh
When to all things here below—I die ;
This flutt'ring pulse, this labouring breath,
And the shadows closing round—are death ;
The veil of the flesh is wearing thin,
And the world beyond is breaking in.
Save, Lord! I sink in this troublous sea ;
I have nothing left but faith in Thee.

I have done with earth—the fear is past,
I've grasp'd the hand of my guide at last ;
And I care not where this robe of clay,
As my spirit drops it, is hid away ;
No terrors now, in the tomb and shroud.
With angel-guards in yon shining cloud,
I rise to my long-desired bourne,
The rest in Jesus, whence none return.

I've done with earth,—with its toil and care,
I have nothing more to do or bear ;
The ear of no earthly friend may know
How sweet within me these musings flow.

To sounds of the spirit-world I wake;
I'm hush'd to the din that mortals make:
Oh Lord! in this hour of mystery,
I have nothing left but faith in Thee.

I've done with earth,—and its nearest ties;
I've faith to think Thou wilt hear the cries
Of those who looked to me as their stay,
Who weep bereft on my dying day.
My tender Father will wipe their tears;
My gracious Saviour will hush their fears;
We're clasping the same Almighty hand,
We meet again in " the better land."

I have done with earth,—have done with sin;
Thou, Lord, hast cleansed my heart within;
Its mighty burden, its daily dross,
Lies there, at the foot of the Holy Cross.
Escaped from the tempter's constant wiles,
To live for ever beneath thy smiles;
No conflict more, and no more distress;
I have pass'd the weary wilderness.

I have done with earth—sad earth—farewell!
I shall not behold what prophets tell;
Thy time of deepening woe and gloom,
Impending curse and ripening doom.
For it draweth on—the awful hour,
The last and worst of Satan's power;
But from his " great wrath" I go to rest,
In calm repose, and on Jesu's breast.

I have done with earth, with the beauty rare,
Which circles its thousand homes so fair;
With its mountain ranges, valleys lone,
And with all the bright sun shines upon.
It hath many caves and dungeons deep,
. Where God doth mark how his children weep;
And where He in flaming fire will make
Inquest for blood, for their dear sake.

I have done with earth till the blessed day,
When I see it new, in fair array;
Till I come again in the countless train
Of the King whose right 'twill be to reign.
When that I now give to the grave to hide,
Shall awake " incorrupt and glorified;"
May mine unclothed spirit accepted be,—
My Lord and Saviour! I sleep in Thee.

1852.

VESPER BELLS

FOR SABBATH EVES.

IF Jesus on this day of rest,
  Hath come into his house of prayer,
And turn'd on every waiting guest,
  His look of love and mildness there;
How must that eye which sees the soul
  Have watch'd each wandering desire!
The sacrifice, or torn or whole,
  The sacred or unhallow'd fire!

Some came bow'd down with worldly care;
  Perchance He took the load away,
And whisper'd, " I myself will bear,
  And do thou only wait and pray!"
Some deeply pierced by broken reeds,
  Fainting, because earth's streams were dried,
Again the Shepherd folds and feeds,
  In Zion by the fountain's side.

He scann'd the depths of every heart.
  " Lovest thou me?" to each he said:
Saw seeming worshippers depart,
  (A congregation of the dead;)

" The dead," with neither life nor love,
    Whom, 'mid disciples mingling there,
Nor mercy wins, nor terrors move,
    " Sent empty" from his house of prayer.

Wast thou " sent empty," oh my soul?
    Had Jesus then no word for thee ?
" The man of sorrows," didst thou frame
    No answer to his " Lov'st thou me "?
If olive-leaves for thee were growing:—
    Say, hast thou pluck'd them by the way?
If still Siloa's brook was flowing ;
    Has thirst of thine been quench'd to-day?

O Lord! " Thou knowest that I love Thee !"
    Wilt Thou not search my heart and see !
If I have idols placed above thee,
    Wilt thou not crush them mightily?
Yet I *do* love Thee, Lord, Thou knowest,
    Heavenly Shepherd—Friend indeed,
Would follow Thee where'er Thou goest,—
    Then give me grace Thy " lambs to feed."

1854.

THE WISDOM OF SILENCE.

THE wisdom of silence is likely to be most forcibly impressed upon us, when we feel that we have unwisely spoken; and it is one of those general heads of reflection under which we may daily add some item earned from experience, some observation harvested from facts and from failures.

The conviction of its truth needs less to be pressed home upon us than the necessity of its practice. Every one allows that there are occasions on which it is wise to be silent. How few, when the occasions arrive, are examples of that which they allow!

It seems that there are two kinds of silence; the one a constitutional bias—stillness, resulting from no effort; the other, an effect of principle, the silence of motive. The latter is, of course, the Christian grace, and referred to in this question; of this it is hard to say whether its nature is active or passive; for, although to be silent is in itself opposed to the action of speech, yet " to refrain the lips," " to bridle the tongue,"—" the tongue which no man can tame," to "quench a fire," to "govern a world of iniquity," are figures employed by inspiration itself, in reference to this apparently negative duty. There is often the strongest mental action in the passive fact of being silent. "If any man offend not in word," says St. James, " the same is a perfect man, and able also to bridle the whole body."

The effect of silence upon the soul itself is salutary. It is the sister of solitude and meditation—invites thought, and gives rest from motion and company. It is an expression towards God of meekness and submission, which, in his sight, are of great price—it is the only attitude of mind meet for the creature in the presence of its Creator—especially when under the corrections of his rod. How shall we reply unto the Lord but with Job, " Behold, I am vile ! what shall I answer thee ? I will lay my hand upon my mouth; once have I spoken, yea twice, but I will proceed no further—but now I will not answer." When the hand of the father is lifted to strike, what remains for the child but to bow ? Nineveh repented in sackcloth and silence, when the vengeance . of Heaven was stayed. " Because thou didst humble thyself before me, when thou heardest my words against thee, and didst rend thy clothes, and weep before me, I have even heard thee, also, saith the Lord."

We have the highest examples of this submission to our Father in heaven in the history of our Redeemer, while on earth. " Thy will be done," was the tacit utterance of his every action; "the cup which my Father hath given me, shall I not drink it ?" And for silence, in given cases, towards our fellow-creatures, we shall likewise find abounding precedents in his perfect life. Whenever our Saviour kept silence, in that silence was wisdom. In the reserves of his omniscience to his followers—" What I do ye know not now, but ye shall know hereafter." In the majesty of his meekness—" when, like a lamb led to the slaughter, he opened not his mouth." In the gentleness of his mercy—when he would not seem to hear the accusing pharisees against the woman convicted of crime, saying only, " Go, and sin no more." May we, in our humble measure, daily seek to imitate him.

Archbishop Leighton has enlarged on the figure of St. Peter, and drawn a map of "that world of iniquity," the tongue. He says, " It hath four quarters, profane speech,

uncharitable speech, vain speech, and double speech." Taunts
and invectives he calls "keen shafts," "the arrows that fly
by day;" railing and slander, "the pestilence that walketh
in darkness." "It is incredible how deep a wound a tongue
sharpened to this work will give—with a very little word and
little noise—like a razor, with a small touch, cutting deep."
Of vain, fruitless speeches, idle, effectless words, he remarks,
"they are the Arabian deserts and barren sands of this
world of evil, the tongue." And of double speech, he adds,
"What of men's speech is not manifestly evil in any of the
other kinds is the most of it naught in this way." Speech,
plausible, fair, but not upright, is what Solomon calls, "silver
dross."

The lips are resembled in Scripture to a door, (Psalm cxli.
3,) and, with some dispositions, this door is always wide open,
affording constant egress to the secrets of others, as well as
their own. However agreeable may be the ready access to
such hearts, it is not safe to deposit treasures in a thorough-
fare;—they must first learn *when* it is wise to be silent, and
sometimes to shut the door.

In circumstances of difficulty and anxiety it is wise to be
silent till we perceive the intimations of Providence. Moses
commanded the Israelites "to stand still and see the salva-
tion of God; the Lord shall fight for you, and ye shall hold
your peace." It is wise to be silent to the suggestions of the
designing and the evil. When the king of Assyria, through
his ambassador, Rabshakeh, mischievously endeavoured to
excite the Jews to rebellion against their monarch, Hezekiah,
by deceitful promises, it is said that the people held their
peace, and answered him not a word; for the king's com-
mandment was, saying, "*Answer him not.*"

It is wise to be silent under reproof, "not answering again."
In this instance, almost without exception, "He that refrain-

eth his lips is wise." We owe it to the Christian profession, if possible, to clear away the stigma of crime; but, otherwise, how, if we cast away the probe, can we expect the wound to be healed?

It is wise to be silent whenever we can *hear* to edification. Silence is wisdom when it bespeaks modesty and humility,— *not* when, by its moveless coldness, it tacitly reproaches all manner of speech. It can alike express the deepest interest, and the most perfect indifference; it often intends acquiescence, yet is frequently a token of dissent; evidently, its wisdom must depend on its occasion; and wise silence is occasional, not continual. It is wise to be silent as to the peculiarities of Christian experience, before those who make a scoff at religion. " Cast not your pearls before swine." King David " kept his mouth with a bridle, and held his peace even from good, while the wicked was before him."

We often expect to find much solace in free and confidential intercourse with a friend, and, after the interview, find it otherwise. It would have been more wise to be silent, and to have spoken with ourselves and with God.

Events occasionally take place in families, which of themselves tend to disunion and jealousy; when these unhappily occur, the wisdom of silence is too seldom observed, which would, in process of time, be the corrective for such evils. Sympathy is sought, and sides are espoused; words repeated, which had better have been buried on the spot where they were uttered. In all such cases, it is certainly wisest for neutral parties, for those who are not required to act, to be silent. They may fetch and carry, without maliciously intending it, a great deal of fuel to the fire; and they will never repent, that, on delicate and difficult questions, they have said too little, and reported nothing.

" Swift to hear, slow to speak;" " In the multitude of

words there wanteth not sin;" "A time to keep silence as well as a time to talk;" are scriptural amulets to wear next our hearts.

It is wise to be silent on the faults of others; when we cannot speak good, not to speak evil. But, alas! the list, as it lengthens, only condemns us; and conscience will be glad to conclude it, in the words of Pharaoh's butler, "I do remember my sins this day."

A mind enveloped in abstraction and reserve, is, nevertheless, neither amiable nor useful. "Out of the abundance of the heart the mouth will speak;" and it is *not* wise to be silent, whenever it is in our power to speak for the glory of God and the good of our fellow-creatures.

It is not wise to be silent to our best friends; it is not wise to be silent at a throne of grace; it is not wise to be silent when principle is at stake: confidence is the soul of friendship, and the heart of a friend should be a sanctuary. If the open and communicative know the evils of their own temperament, they will choose for their intimates the silent and reserved. Whether for example or safety's sake, wisdom is more than knowledge. Most of us know when it is wise to be silent; the wisdom of silence is the practice of that knowledge.

JUBILEE ODE.

A SEQUEL TO "THE BOOK AND ITS STORY."

When Thou, O God! went'st forth in time of old,
  And riding on the cloud,
Unto thy flock—encamp'd in desert fold—
  Thy might and glory bow'd;
At seraph utterance of thy solemn word,
  The giant buttresses of Sinai stirr'd;
And now the voice that shook those ancient hills
The circle of the wide creation fills!

In thunder-tones to trembling Israel
  Did God first give the word;
In after years from prophet-harps inspired,
  The Spirit's voice was heard:
And then, Jehovah-Lord, to human ear,
Gently and unperceived thou didst draw near,—
Thy mighty Godhead robed in earthly veil,—
And left Evangelists to tell the tale.

Thy chariots, myriads of angels be—
  They utter'd first the word:
Since then upon how great a company
  Is the same gift conferr'd!

And as of yore did hoary Sinai bow,
The whole earth moves to meet thy presence now :
Wide, and yet wider still each opening morn
The solemn witness of thy word is borne.

List! for the Jubilate long and loud
   Beginneth from the Isles,
Where Cambria's barren rocks first craved the word,
   And now, the Gospel smiles.
Though still the ruin'd fortress crowns her steeps,
For savage war and crime no more she weeps,
But all her mountain-air she gladly fills
With silver voices from her ancient rills.

As feed those many rills her noble streams,
   Rushing through rock and glen,
From thousand cottage-homes Britannia pours
   The word of life to men :
And whilst her happy island-influence rides
All round the world the surging ocean tides,
Benighted denizens of farthest seas
Begin to mingle in her Jubilees!

Rome trembles at the mighty word she hid
   In her own cloister'd cells;
The failing followers of Islàm forbid
   In vain, the truths it tells ;
And in its ancient seats and antique founts
Again the pure and living water mounts,
Prepared o'er each green marge to spread and flow,
And help to bid the world Christ's empire know.

Churches of God! that yet are holding fast
  The "faithful word" in "love,"
Forget your long disunion in the past,
  And parties rise above!
In love come forth! for see! the heathen wait
Your patient guidance to yon pearly gate:
The heathen know that by your hand is given
To them the " sacred letter fresh from heaven."

In Britain's glorious year of Jubilee,
  Lo! China pleads her want;
A million of those wingèd words of life
  We hasten swift to grant:
India awakes! and half the darksome earth
Springs instant to a new and nobler birth;
Soon shall the healing leaves of life's fair tree
Scatter'd through all the waiting nations be.

And surely as we thus " prepare His way,"
  And sow the precious seed,
We soon shall mark the dawn of brighter day,—
  The Jubilee indeed !
When He whose only right it is to reign,
Unto his earthly kingdom comes again;
And then, oh Holy Father, Spirit, Son!
On earth, in heaven, shall " Thy will be done!"

1853.

NINEVEH AND ITS RELICS

IN THE BRITISH MUSEUM.

I.

COME back, come back into the past!
   The ancient Ages call;
Sennacherib bids his guests once more,
   Enter his palace-hall—
Colossal forms[1] the portals guard,
And long the entrance hath been barr'd.

II.

Not from Assyria's sandy plains,
   The wond'ring throng sweeps in,
But out of London's mighty heart,
   Its moving life and din,
We press to seek the calm sublime,
Fresh risen from the tomb of time.

III.

The avenging God by "fire" and "flood,"[2]
   Fulfilling Nahum's word;
The city that was stain'd with blood,
   For Israel's sake abhorr'd,[3]
Cast down, in pagan pomp and pride,
'Neath mounds of dust, in shame to hide.

IV.

Thousands of years have sped away ;
  And now these sculptures stand,
Forth to a world that is grown grey,
  Carved by its childish hand ;
Long o'er their grave the Arab trod,[4]
Lost and forgotten—save by God.

V.

Grim Nisroch[5] and his priestly train
  Rise from their stony bed ;
The Idols see the light again !
  Th' adorers all are dead !
When Israel sought to gods of clay,[6]
These heathen cherubim were they.

VI.

Rare fragile ivory ornaments ![7]
  Ye touch the heart to tears,
Come up to speak from the dark " pit,"[8]
  Buried three thousand years !
The crumblings of earth's oldest throne,[9]
Which God had said should be o'erthrown.

VII.

Fair antique lamps, as if just quench'd !
  Glass, opal-dyed by age,
Dim fragment-links 'twixt Now and Then,
  Ye lead to nobler page,
" Kings' archives "[10]—where in mystic heap
Lost histories of nations sleep.

VIII.

For Thee, thou one mute worshipper[11]
  Of the vast idols round,
Lone remnant of humanity
  In the burnt palace found,
Thy tale, alas! may ne'er be read,
Till Nineveh shall yield its dead.

IX.

And why, by God's own hand unseal'd
  In this appointed hour,
Why now are these rude forms reveal'd?
  And whence hath science power
Afresh to scan this arrowy tongue,
In silence sepulchred so long?

X.

Caves, mounds, and written mountains[12] hide
  In libraries of stone,
At God's good pleasure to restore,
  The proofs which all shall own,
That the " sure word of prophecy "
Abideth everlastingly.

XI.

And deep within earth's quiet breast,
  On many an eastern plain,
Yet mightier secrets still may rest,
  That shall God's word explain;
High records for deciphering hand,
The lore of Abraham's father-land.

XII.

" Thou shalt be hid" [13]—that word declared,
  And now that thou art found,
What voice to us, oh Nineveh!
  Floats from thy funeral mound?
" As were fulfill'd God's threats to ME,[14]
So shall his future threatenings be.

XIII.

" I, with my graven images,[15]
  Went down into the dust,
Ere men had their Redeemer seen,—
  ' The holy one,—the just.'
If I at Jonah's preaching turn'd,
What had I from the Saviour learn'd?

XIV.

" I clasp'd the keys of bygone years
  In long and dreamless sleep,
And lay, till God should call me forth,
  Entranced in chambers deep ;
He bids me prove how true the past,
On a future age a gleam to cast.

XV.

" For my idols all will see the day,
  When ' Greater Babylon'
My archetype—shall, swept away,[16]
  Make room for ' the Mighty One,'—
For Him ' whom all nations and peoples shall
    praise,' [17]
Whose throne is ' set up by the Ancient of Days.'

XVI.

" Intenser fires shall light the earth,
 Than mine,—when God ' destroys'
With burning breath the ' man of sin,'[18]
 And his last and strongest lies ;
The stone of His kingdom of truth to lay,[19]
The kingdom that ' never shall pass away.' "

XVII.

Come back, come back into the past !
 The ancient Ages call—
Come muse upon Time and Eternity,
 In Sennacherib's palace-hall :
Colossal forms the portals guard,
And long the entrance hath been barr'd.

NOTES AND REFERENCES TO NINEVEH.

Verse 1.

[1] " *Colossal forms.*"

The winged, human-headed lions and bulls which kept the gates of the
Assyrian temples ; the likeness between which and the forms seen by
Ezekiel in his vision, is too striking not to be noticed. The prophet had
been a captive in the land of Assyria. The book of Daniel (who was also
familiar with the Assyrian sacred types) teems with descriptions of these
curious animal and human combinations.

" Where is the dwelling of the lions, and the feeding-place of the
young lions, where the lion, even the old lion, walked, and the lion's
whelp—and none made them afraid ?

" The lion did tear in pieces enough for his whelps, and strangled for
his lionesses, and filled his holes with prey, and his dens with ravin."
(Nahum ii. 11, 12.)

The above is a noble description of the violent and warlike character
of the Assyrian kings, whose palaces appear to have been also the temples
of their gods.

VERSE 3.

¹ " *The avenging God by fire and flood.*"

" For while they shall be folden together as thorns, and while they are
drunken as drunkards, they shall be devoured as stubble fully dry." (Nahum i. 10.)

" The palace shall be dissolved (as in margin) molten." (Nahum ii. 6.)

" Behold, I am against thee, saith the Lord of Hosts, and I will burn
her chariots in the smoke, and the sword shall devour thy young lions ;
and I will cut off thy prey from the earth, and the voice of thy messen-
gers shall no more be heard." (Nahum ii. 13.)

" The gates of thy land shall be set wide open unto thine enemies ; the
fire shall devour thy bars." (Nahum iii. 13.)

" Then shall the fire devour thee." (Nahum iii. 15.)

" Flood."

" But with an over-running flood He will make an utter end of the
place thereof." (Nahum i. 8.)

" The gates of the rivers shall be opened." (Nahum ii. 6.)

VERSE 3.

² " *The city that was stain'd with blood,*
For Israel's sake abhorr'd."

" Woe to the bloody city ! it is full of lies and robbery." (Nahum iii. 1.)

" For now I will break his yoke from off thee, I will burst thy bands
in sunder." (Nahum i. 13.)

" The Jews paid tribute to the Assyrians, (see 2 Kings xviii. 14,) and
the Israelites were under actual captivity among them at the time of this
prophecy." (Newcome " on the Minor Prophets.")

The same commentator observes, that " this prophecy was highly interesting to the Jews, as the Assyrians had often ravaged their country,
and had recently destroyed the kingdom of Israel." (p. 173.)

"The prophecy of Nahum was uttered about 713 B.C., shortly before the victorious army of Sennacherib was smitten by the angel of Jehovah." (Isa. xxxvii. 36.) It must have been to the believing Hebrews of that age, in some measure what the Apocalypse was to the early Christians,— a ground of assurance that the people of God should ultimately triumph in the great conflict with the powers of darkness in which they were then engaged.

The city of Nineveh had fallen in the year 606 B.C. In the year 588 B.C., the prophet Ezekiel, in his 31st chapter, speaks of the Assyrian power as destroyed, which it had been about twenty-four years previously to his prophecy.

VERSE 4.

⁴ "*Long o'er their grave the Arab trod.*"

"I will make thy grave; for thou art vile." (Nahum i. 14.)

"And I will cast abominable filth upon thee, and will make thee vile, and will set thee as a gazing-stock." (Nahum iii. 6.)

VERSE 5.

⁵ "*Grim Nisroch and his priestly train.*"

Nisr signifies, in all Semitic languages, an eagle;—the eagle-headed deity is prominent among the Assyrian sculptures. Biblical scholars, long before the discoveries of Mr. Layard, had concluded that in the Assyrian Pantheon the chief god was worshipped under the form of an eagle.

"So Sennacherib, the king of Assyria, dwelt at Nineveh. And it came to pass, as he was worshipping in the house of Nisroch his god, that his sons smote him with the sword." (2 Kings xix. 37.)

⁶ "*When Israel sought to gods of clay.*"

"And they followed vanity, and became vain, and went after the heathen that were round about them, concerning whom the Lord had charged them that they should not do like them." (2 Kings xviii. 15.)

"For Ahaz took away a portion out of the house of the Lord, and out of the house of the king, and of the princes, and gave it unto the king of Assyria; but he helped him not. And in the time of his distress did he trespass yet more against the Lord; this is that king Ahaz. For he sacrificed unto the gods of Darmesek, which smote him : and he said, Because the gods of the kings of Assyria help them, therefore will I sacrifice unto them, that they may help me. But they were the ruin of him, and of all Israel." (2 Chron. xxviii. 21–23.)

" These heathen cherubim were they."

" With cherubim of cunning work made he them." (Exod. xxxvi. 8.)

What these cherubim were cannot be determined. Josephus, in his Antiquities of the Jews, says, " they were flying animals like none of those which are seen by man, but such as Moses saw about the throne of God." These symbolical figures, according to the description given of them by Ezekiel, were creatures with four heads and one body, and the animals of which these forms consisted were the noblest of their kind: the lion among wild beasts, the bull among tame ones, the eagle among the birds, and man at the head of all; so that they might be, says Dr. Priestley, the representatives of all nature. Hence some have conceived them to be somewhat of the shape of flying oxen. This seems to have been the ancient opinion which tradition had handed down concerning the shape of the cherubim with the flaming sword that guarded the tree of life. (Genesis iii. 26.)—*See* Note to Exodus xxxvi. 8, in Bagster's " Comprehensive Bible."

That the Assyrians should have derived the idea (which these vast stony forms are come forth to express to us after their long and solemn sleep in the depths of the earth) from the golden cherubim of the ark of God, and yet further, from the cherubim which guarded the gate of Eden, invests them with unspeakable interest.

VERSE 6.

⁷ *" Rare fragile ivory ornaments."*

This verse and part of the seventh refers to a single, and most interesting case of relics from Nineveh. Ivory ornaments, supposed to be those of the throne, falling to pieces on coming in contact with the air, have been boiled in isinglass to restore their tenacity, at the suggestion of Professor Owen. They are exceedingly curious and beautiful.

⁸ *" Come up to speak from the dark pit."*

The whole of the 31st chapter of Ezekiel deserves to be studied with
6

attention in reference to the destruction of Nineveh. It is too long for quotation entire. The passage commences, " Behold, the Assyrian was like a cedar in Lebanon," &c. Nothing can be more natural than that the prophet should warn Pharaoh, the Egyptian monarch, by the example of the Assyrian empire, which had been destroyed twenty-four years previously to the delivery of this prophecy by the very same prince (Nebuchadnezzar), who, within twenty years more, was to conquer Egypt. (Horsley's " Biblical Criticism.")

" For they are all delivered unto death, to the nether parts of the earth, in the midst of the children of men, with them that go down to the pit. Thus saith the Lord God; In the day when he went down to the grave I caused a mourning. I made the nations to shake at the sound of his fall." (Ezekiel xxxi. 14–16.)

9 " *Earth's oldest throne.*"

Within a century after the flood, and while Noah was in the full vigour of his power, his great grandson Nimrod is introduced on the historic page as the founder of Nineveh: " Out of the land of Shinar, he went into Assyria (as marginal reading), and builded Nineveh." (Genesis x.)

Verse 7.

10 " *King's archives.*"

The visitor to the Museum should not neglect to seek for the upper room in which the Babylonian and Assyrian bricks, inscribed with arrowheaded characters, are to be found, and which the learned are now so busily and successfully deciphering.

" The palace of Nineveh has evidently been destroyed by fire, but one portion of the building seemed to have escaped its influence, and Mr. Layard found a large room filled with what appeared to be the Archives of the Empire, ranged in successive tablets of Terra Cotta, the writing being as perfect as when the tablets were first stamped. They were piled in huge heaps from the floor to the ceiling; this chamber, Major Rawlinson thought might be presumed to be the house of records of the Assyrian Kings. When these tablets had been deciphered, he believed that we should have a better acquaintance with the history, the religion, the philosophy, and the jurisprudence of Assyria 1500 years before the Christian era, than we had of Greece or Rome during any period of their respective histories."

Verse 8.

[11] *" For thee—thou one mute worshipper."*

In the case of fragment ivories, is one human skull, evidently that of a young person from the beauty of the teeth, and it is said to be the only one found in the burnt palace.

Verse 10.

[12] *" Caves, mounds, and written mountains, hide."*

This is an allusion to the Sinaitic Inscriptions on the rocks and cliffs of the Wady Mokkateb, or Written Valley, now believed by many to have been the work of the children of Israel whilst wandering in the wilderness, and which are being copied and deciphered with much care and pains after the lapse of ages.—*See* Rev. C. Forster's " Voice of Israel from the rocks of Sinai."

" The sure word of prophecy."

" We have also a more sure word of prophecy, whereunto ye do well that ye take heed, *as unto a light that shineth in a dark place*, until the day dawn, and the day-star arise in your hearts." (2 Peter i. 19.)

Verse 12.

[13] *" Thou shalt be hid, that word declared."*

" Thou shalt be hid." (Nahum iii. 11.)

" As were fulfill'd God's threats to Me."

" The gates of the rivers shall be opened." Most remarkably was this accomplished. We are told by Diodorus, that in his plans for the defence of the city, the King of Assyria was greatly encouraged by an ancient prophecy—*That Nineveh should never be taken until the river became its enemy*—but that after the allied revolters had besieged the city for two years without effect, there occurred a prodigious inundation of the Tigris, when the stream overflowed its banks and rose up to the city, and swept away about twenty furlongs of its great wall. When the king heard this unexpected fulfilment of the old prediction, he was filled with consternation and despair; he gave up all for lost: and that he might not fall into

the hands of his enemies, he caused a large pile of wood to be raised in
his palace, and, heaping thereon all his gold and silver and apparel, and
collecting his eunuchs and concubines, ordered the pile to be set on fire,
whereby all those persons, with himself, his treasures, and his palace were
utterly consumed. The inundation of the Tigris was probably caused by
the melting of the snows in the mountains of Armenia. A similar cir-
cumstance occurred a few years since in Bagdad, the greatest city that
now exists on the same river."

"In which of the palaces Sardanapalus burnt himself with his wives
and followers is not ascertained. It is remarkable, that while no one has
yet discovered a burnt temple in Egypt or Greece, all these Assyrian
palaces have been destroyed by fire; the slabs lining the chambers bear
certain marks of it. A considerable quantity of coal, and even pieces of
half-burnt wood were found in many places; and it must have been a violent and prolonged fire—to calcine not only a few spots—but every part
of the slabs ten feet high, and several inches thick. So complete a
decomposition can be attributed only to intense heat, such as would be
occasioned by the fall of a burning roof. Not a single bas-relief capable
of preservation was found in any of the chambers at Khorsabad; they
were all pulverized. Those on the outside, on the contrary, were in a
good state of preservation."

Verse 13.

[14] "*I and my graven images*
Went down into the dust."

"Confounded be all they that serve graven images." (Ps. xcvii. 7.)

Verse 15.

[15] "*When 'Greater Babylon,'*
My archetype—shall, swept away,"

"And the kings of the earth shall bewail her and lament for her, when
they shall see the smoke of her burning, standing afar off for the fear of
her torment, saying, Alas, alas, that great city Babylon, that mighty
city! for in one hour is thy judgment come." (Rev. xviii. 9, 10.)

"For in one hour is she made desolate." (Rev. xviii. 19.)

"And after these things I saw another angel come down from heaven,
having great power; and the earth was lightened with his glory.

" And he cried mightily with a strong voice, saying, Babylon the great is fallen ; is fallen, and is become the habitation of devils, and the hold of every foul spirit, and a cage of every unclean and hateful bird.

" And I heard another voice from heaven, saying, Come out of her, my people, that ye be not partakers of her sins, and that ye receive not of her plagues." (Rev. xviii. 1, 2.)

Verse 15.

17 " For Him whom all nations and peoples shall praise."

" I beheld then because of the great words which the horn spake, I beheld even till the beast was slain, and his body destroyed, and given to the burning flame.

" And, behold, one like the Son of man came with the clouds of heaven, and came to the Ancient of days, and they brought him near before him.

" And there was given him dominion, and glory, and a kingdom, that al' people, nations, and languages, should serve Him; his dominion is an everlasting dominion, which shall not pass away, and his kingdom that which shall not be destroyed." (Daniel vii. 13, 14.)

Verse 16.

18 " The ' Man of Sin,'
And his last and strongest lies."

" Let no man deceive you by any means, for that day shall not come, except there come a falling away first, and that Man of Sin be revealed, the Son of perdition ; who opposeth and exalteth himself above all that is called God, or that is worshipped, so that he as God sitteth in the temple of God, shewing himself that he is God." (2 Thess. ii. 3, 4.)

" Thou shalt take up this proverb against the king of Babylon, and say, How hath the oppressor ceased ! the golden city ceased ! " (Isaiah xiv. 4.)

" How art thou fallen from heaven, O Lucifer, Son of the morning! For thou hast said in thine heart, I will ascend into heaven, I will exalt my throne above the stars of God. I will ascend above the heights of the clouds ; I will be like the Most High. Yet thou shalt be brought down to hell, to the sides of the pit." (Isaiah xiv. 12–15.)

" In the year that king Ahaz died was this burden." (Isaiah xiv. 28.) B.C. 712.

" For the mystery of iniquity doth already work; only He who now

letteth will let, until he be taken out of the way. And then shall that
Wicked be revealed, whom the Lord shall consume with the spirit of his
mouth, and shall destroy with the brightness of his coming: Even him,
whose coming is after the working of Satan with all power and signs and
lying wonders, and with all deceivableness of unrighteousness in them
that perish; because they received not the love of the truth, that they
might be saved. And for this cause God shall send them strong delu-
sion, that they should believe a lie." (2 Thess. ii. 7–11.)

[19] "*The stone of his kingdom of truth to lay.*"

" Thou, O king, sawest till that a stone was cut out without hands,
which smote the image upon his feet that were of iron and clay, and
brake them to pieces. Then was the iron, the clay, the brass, the silver,
and the gold, broken to pieces together, and became like the chaff of the
summer threshing-floors; and the wind carried them away, that no place
was found for them: and the stone that smote the image became a great
mountain, and filled the whole earth." (Daniel ii. 34, 35.)   "And in the
days of these kings, shall the God of heaven set up a kingdom which
shall never be destroyed; and the kingdom shall not be left to other
people, but it shall break in pieces and consume all these kingdoms, and
it shall stand for ever." (Daniel ii. 44.)

" Therefore thus saith the Lord God, Behold, I lay in Zion for a foundation a stone, a tried stone, a precious corner-stone, a sure foundation—
Judgment also will I lay to the line, and righteousness to the plummet;
and the hail shall sweep away the refuge of lies." (Isaiah xxviii. 16, 17.
Rev. xvi. 19–21.)

" The stone which the builders refused is become the headstone of the
corner." (Psalm cxviii. 22.)

" Thy kingdom come. Thy will be done in earth, as it is in heaven."

N.B.—Many of the foregoing quotations are to be found in a very
interesting volume entitled " Nineveh and its Palaces." (*National Illustrated Library.*)

LEAVES

IS THINE THE LYRE?

Is thine the lyre?—the poet's lyre?
  Has Heaven made thine heart,
Deeply and quietly desire,
  All nature can impart?
Is it a home of sympathies
  For simple and sublime?
An urn of precious memories,
  Laid up from long past time?
Oh! never seek for wealth or power,
Such heart alone is richer dower.

Is thine the lyre? Does music's tone
  Come thrilling through thy breast,
Not with the gush of song alone,
  In melody express'd,
But utter'd by all silent things—
  All images of rest—
Heard in the hush which evening sings,
  To lull the fiery west?
If such thy soul's harmonious shrine,
Then all the wealth of *sound* is thine.

Is thine the lyre? When roaming free
   O'er mountain, heath, and dell,
Seest thou treasures stored for thee
   In cup, and bud, and bell?
Gather from these thy gold and gems,
   And in the moonlight's glow,
For silver, to the birchen stems,
   Go! to the deep woods go!
Tread every step of nature's throne,
All *sights* of beauty are thine own!

Is thine the lyre? Its master chords
   In human hearts are heard,
When love or grief, as sovereign lords,
   Affection's depths have stirr'd.
But childhood's smile can music make,
   At any hour, to thee;
From youth's dark eyes a light doth break
   Of deeper witchery.
Age in thy sight all winning seems,
A poet's life has lovely dreams.

Is thine the lyre? I deem the shell
   Was in thy cradle found.
Art can but imitate its swell,
   And mock its native sound.
In early days, with weal or woe
   Unsought, its whispers came,
Unconsciously, with feeling's flow;
   And still they come, the same.

Through life alone thou ne'er can'st wend,
The lyre for thy familiar friend.

Is thine the lyre ?   In still retreats
  Go l feed its sacred fire ;
Forsake the din of crowded streets,
  Indulge thy soul's desire:
She seeks the lofty and the calm,
  The beautiful, the old ;
Aspires—and craves serene delights,
  Meet for her purer mould.
But noise, and care, and common things,
Are weights upon her radiant wings.

And yet, in paths of upper air,
  Thou need'st not ever stray ;
For haunted realms of poesy
  Border life's beaten way.
There's not a heath so brown and bare,
  But morning gems with dew !
Nor human lot so scantly fair,
  But to thy gifted view
Shall yield some element of fire
To touch thy heart, and tone thy lyre.

Is thine the lyre? Then God who gave
  To thee these gentle powers
To press ethereal essence out
  From many unseen flowers ;
Whilst for thy joy their odour fleets,
  Claims that thy lyre should bring

To Him who fill'd earth's lap with sweets,
    Its tribute offering.
Thy lyre hath strings of Heaven's tone,
Let Heaven its cadence ne'er disown.

1833.

ON SOME MOSSES, FERNS, AND MOSS-INSECTS,

SEEN THROUGH A MICROSCOPE OF HIGH POWER.

IT was not all a tale of eld,
That fairies, who their revels held
By moonlight, in the greenwood shade
Their beakers of the moss-cups made.
The wond'rous light which science burns,
Reveals those lovely jewell'd urns!
Fair lace-work spreads from roughest stems,
And shews each tuft a mine of gems.
    Voices from the silent sod,
    Speaking of the Perfect God!

Urns of beauty—forms of glory—
Shapes with frosted silver hoary;
Fair cups of light, that pearls enfold,
Set in transparent gauzy gold;
Lucid sprays of emerald dye,
Could e'en an empire's jewels vie

With all these groupes of gems that burn
On each separate frond of fern?
   Voices from the silent sod,
   Speaking of the Perfect God!

Fringeless, or fringed, and fringed again,
No single leaflet form'd in vain ;
What wealth of heavenly wisdom lies
Within one moss-cup's mysteries !
And few may know what silvery net,
Down in its mimic depths is set,
To catch the rarest dews that fall
Upon the dry and barren wall.
   Voices from the silent sod,
   Speaking of the Perfect God!

Tiny, flame-like, living creatures,
With your varying starry features,
Travellers in this waste of glory,
With no tongue to tell its story,
Here ye abide—and nectar sip,
Oft tasting every ruby tip.
Possess ye microscopic eyes,
Exploring all these mysteries?
   Ye are voices from the sod,
   Speaking of the Perfect God!

If the crystal man hath moulded,
Such delight hath now unfolded,
What radiant wealth of glad surprise
Will surely wait our ravish'd eyes,

As they, restored to primal power,
Find " the new earth" to be their dower.
And when, redeem'd from mortal care,
With the bright angels we shall hear,
  Voice alike from star and sod,
  Speaking of the Perfect God !

1851.

STAFFA.

How loud the voice of storms must sound
  By night, in Fingal's cave !
The sea-birds hear it—hear around
  The wild winds mourn and rave.
It is not meet for mortal ear,
Man hath not made his dwelling near.

We come in calms—with summer tides,
  This long-drawn aisle explore,
When the small skiff securely glides
  Upon its emerald floor;
And wond'ring tread its giant stair
In sunlight, when the heavens are fair.

Short glimpses, else the waves possess
  The temple they have worn;
And roll their loud and lonely bass
  Through the dark arch in scorn:

As glorying that none shall share
In their Creator's worship there.

Oh! lavish wealth of power divine,
    This wond'rous world contains;
Which veil'd, as in this ocean shrine,
    Age after age remains;
And seemeth in its shroud sublime,
Link 'twixt Eternity and Time.

1834.

THE HOME OF THE SHARK.

AN OCEAN VIVARIUM.

A MONSTER'S home, and yet no darksome den,
He made his palace in an ocean glen,
Most fair, and far retired in southern seas;
And Staffa's isle in the old Hebrides
Rears not its arch of basalt from a floor
So richly paven.
                    The same sun doth pour
Into the depths of each lone cave his ray,
Waking to crimson, violet, gold, and grey,
The solemn grandeur of their fretted walls,
As is his wont in Neptune's secret halls,
And those alone.   And the same moon at night
Filleth their silence with her silver light;

Piercing the smooth green waters that have found
A place of rest, in rocky girdle bound.
I ken the wealth of Staffa, but I deem,
More like the scenery of a fairy dream,
This nameless cavern.
                        From the roof depending
Long stalactites, with pearly points descending,
Of strangest forms—reflect them in a tide
So pure, so still, that all the garden wide
Of beauty, which those calm depths treasure, lies
As in enchanted slumber.   Here, from root
Of crimson coral, springs a feathery shoot
Of vegetable life—tall, delicately fine !
And to the surface tending ; there, entwine
In tracery round each rocky point, a net
Of fibres of all hues, in which is set
Ofttimes the ocean fan.   A column shaft
The pale green stem of fucus doth enwaft ;
Another ocean plant, has broad leaves shed
Across a rocky arch.   While drooping red
From shelving ledge, a thousand more impinge.
A Nereid's bower ! and 'mid such verdant fringe,
Arauna, Teira, Cheotodon, straying,
With silvery vest, and stripes of azure playing,
People the coral reefs : oft chasing far
The dark slow Corie, and the golden Star.
But mark—those rocks a dark abyss disclose :
Into such world of beauty sudden rose
Wolf of the waters—gurgling, glaring round—
A shark enormous !
                *   *   *   *   *

1835.

I LOVE TO BE ALONE.

I LOVE to be alone at twilight's fall,
And watch the shadows stealing over all—
Night's voiceless heralds! silently they claim
Dominion in her dark and gentle name,
And mass in grey whate'er of daylight's pride
Her diadem of gems might dim or hide.

The light before them fleets, and in its train,
Colour and form ;—till nought distinct remain,
Save earth and sky.   Now gentle moon, arise,
And ride in beauty up those calmèd skies !
Smile through the aspen foliage, frail and light,
Silver the graceful sheaves in quiet might ;
Scatter the fleecy clouds upon thy way !
Glance on the woods, and, emulous of day,
Restore their green beneath thy glittering ray !

Fair orb, of lustre mild ! to broken hearts
Thy pale reflected light a balm imparts.
Long hath thy beam had power to soothe the sad,
For whom the sunny noontide was too glad :
Emblem of peace ! the peace of heaven above thee ;
All love thee, gentle moon ! the lonely love thee.
Lighting like cheerful friend, their silent cot ;
And lovers love thee—Ah ! who loves thee not ?

Wert thou not link'd of old with vow and token?
Vows kept and broken—Thou didst hear them spoken!

I love thee, gentle moon! although no thrill
Of tumult, at this hour, my spirit fill;
No anxiousness of love—that aching guest,
Nor melancholy, wakes its happy rest.
I love thee for thine own sweet sake, and deem
The clouds, drinking thy pure and sparkling beam,
Are like the griefs thou'rt lightening on thy way;
But hist! I hear those distant voices say,
'Tis strange that lonesome paths I choose behind,
While up the hill so merrily they wind.

I love your converse sweet, and lightsome play;
Yet better, better love, to steal away
At such an hour as this, from mirthful tone;
At twilight's fall—I love to be alone.

1831.

RAIN UPON THE MOUNTAINS.

BEN CRUACHAN.

KNOW ye the silence of the mountain side,
Before the clouds that fleece its summit fall
In silver showers? only the rill doth call
To warn the small birds in their nests to hide.
Then is the sunbeam for a season fled,
Then bursts the storm upon the harebell's head,
And round about in robe of mist doth ride.
That robe is rending—mark! intensest glow
Of colour on the shadowy crags hath birth;
The bow is born upon the mountain's brow,
The hues of heaven are rising from the earth,
Gray cairns have caught the tone, and dark pine stems,
The purple heather drips with iris gems;
Oh! fairer for her frown, is nature's mirth.

1834.

7

THE CAVES OF PLEMONT, JERSEY.

YES! thou art glorious, thou deep green sea!
Thou cradlest all the earth on thy broad breast;
Her far-spread continents are isles to thee;
Her isles thy playthings—which thou lovest best,
When thou hast worn thyself a home of rest
Such as in Cesarea's rocky walls;
Winning thy way round pinnacle and crest
Into the crag's dark heart, where venturous falls
The foot of man, but while the tide retires;—
And then with broad and mighty sweep, thy choirs
Of sounding billows, in their sevenfold strength,
Pronounce all mortal trace effaced at length,
And as they gently kiss their palace floor,
Proclaim it as their own for evermore.

1853.

COLUMBUS TO THE INDIAN.

" In this great man's first voyage of discovery, 1492, having explored
St. Salvador and Cuba, he was proceeding to Hayti, when the ship over-
took a single Indian in a canoe. He had a mere morsel of bread and
a calabash of water, with a string of glass beads, such as they had given
at St. Salvador, shewing he came from thence; and was probably
passing from island to island to give notice of the ships. Columbus
admired the hardihood of this simple voyager, making such an extensive
expedition in so frail a bark. He took him and his canoe on board, fed
him, and landed him with abundance of presents."—*Life of Christopher
Columbus, by Washington Irving.*

HAIL to thee, kindred spirit, the fearless and the free!
Alone and unattended, tracking the ocean sea.
From far thy little bark I have anxiously espied,
A speck upon the waters, and now thou'rt by my side.

As the " white men from heaven," thou hast heard of us
          before,
That string of beads was brought from a distant island
          shore ;
And having heard the wonder—thy little sail unfurl'd,
From isle to isle thou'rt passing, to tell it to thy world!

Nay, tender not thy treasure, for a " wampum-belt" of
          peace ;
'Tis needless, till my trust in thy simple faith shall cease.
Thy morsel, and thy calabash, thy little bark and thee,
Will ne'er be harm'd or spoil'd, or seized upon by me.

'Tis true our language differs; I hear thee not in words
Give utterance to the impulse that sweeps thy spirit's
          chords;
But thy dark eye flashes enterprise, and from its light
          alone,
I can tell thy heart beats high, with feelings like my own!

Thou must have felt ere now, how proud it is to be
The first that treads new lands, beyond the rolling sea.
Ah, who of all my civilised, of all my dastard train,
Had ever dared, as thou hast done, to plough the unknown
          main?

No; they are cold and heartless, their ardour ever failing;
And ever, at the thought of ill, their woman-courage
          quailing;
While at me the darts of treachery and mutiny are hurl'd;
Though guiding them to conquest and possession of a
          world!

Thou art one of the noble few to be found in every clime,
Whose daring intellect outstrips their dark and bigot time;
Who in joy, but most in sorrow, by land, or on the sea,
Do ever hold communion, and such I hold with thee!

A DISCOURSE

WITH A COPY OF WORDSWORTH'S POEMS,

ON ITS RETURN FROM THE STUDY OF MR. C. N. D., TO WHOM IT HAD BEEN LENT FOR A MONTH.

WELL, Wordsworth, and so here thou art again,
My joy and treasure! Since we parted, I
Have met none like thee, Nature's priest! Declare
What welcome has been given thine excellence
By him to whom I sent thee?—Reverence due
Has genius paid to genius?

WORDSWORTH.

A welcome slight; and reverence not at all;
Why did you send me? He did not invite,
Nor has he understood. Why wish'd you me
To breathe such learnèd air? and how could you
Expect me to receive reception better,
As not being written in Greek, or in Black Letter?

Master and friend,—I pray, forgive thy pupil!
" He has not understood?" I sent thee, sure,
To one who aught he chose could understand.

WORDSWORTH.

He did not choose, then, me to understand.
Not being an old book; and he hates moderns,
One and all.   E'en my outside pleased him not;
And for the spirit that doth in me dwell,
He did not seek it; 'twas not worth his while:
He only stalks with Milton's majesty,
And cannot stoop to note the weeds that broider
Life's daily path.

He did not like thine outside, thinkest thou?
Thou 'rt bound like an old Missal, as he said,
Himself; I heard him.

WORDSWORTH.

　　　　All the worse for that
In his eyes.—Popery, I find, he hates;
And e'en conformity in least degrees,
Down to a gown and bands! No pulpit-cushion
Indeed for him.   " Wood and the word" alone.
In Politics we two should never meet;
How dream'd you that we should? these, principles
He calls,—I, prejudices.

I sent thee not to him for Politics,
But for the sake of holier Poesy;
His converse with the spirits of old time,
And the calm grandeur of their quiet thoughts,

Had made him more thy friend ; 'tis with their eye
Thou hast look'd forth on common homely things,
Ennobling e'en the meanest of them all.
I sent thee, that thy fresh delight in nature
Might make a green place in his soul, a spot
For sunbeams here and there, among the steeps
Of lofty science, such as thou hast made
For lesser minds, amid life's daily cares.
Could'st thou not win him to thy mountain haunts,
With voice of rills? what, not with thy "Recluse"
Could he find tranquil sympathies?

WORDSWORTH.

At least
He would not; for more sweet than mountain air,
The noxious fragrance of Virginian leaf,
He deemeth ever; and its fuming wreaths
Compose him to serenest meditation.
He hath no need of me.

Thou hast not tried thy moral power on him ;
He loves simplicity, and kindliness
Of nature meets in him with kindliness
Responsive ; Thou dost " love each living thing,
And every flower that blows "—the last and best
Accomplishment of greatest minds! He feels,
As thou would'st feel, life's tend'rest charities,
Indulgence not unmeet for mental strength.
Met ye not, even here?

WORDSWORTH.

We have *not* met; nay, heed it not too much;
We may, some future time; when, in an hour
Of summer leisure, he shall cast aside
His learnèd lore awhile, unconsciously,
To feel with me.　I own him of the few
Whom I would care to claim as votaries.
My voice was lost amid those foreign tongues;
But in the green-wood he will hear me still.
The vulgar heed me not; the great contemn;
The witty ridicule.　I pass these by,
And find my home in lowly, loving hearts,
Here and there one.　Wherever nature flings
Her treasures, are my soul's possessions,
And all who love *her* are my children;
I can afford, at first, to be despised.

1836.

A LETTER FROM A NORWOOD GIPSY.

WRITTEN FOR A FANCY SALE FOR THE NORWOOD SCHOOLS.

So, Mortal, thou art come
To learn of me thy doom;
And what is hid for thee
In dim futurity;
Come, cross my hand with gold,
Ere its secrets can be told.

When the moon her cycle fills,
Amid these haunted hills,
(For ages past our home,)
My wizard sisters roam,
And scan with coal-black eye
The cyphers of the sky;
I ween those cyphers be
As dark to them as thee.

In solemn woods to stray,
I love no less than they;
But of late, I own 'tis true,
I've found something else to do.
Tho' I hate to live by rule,
Yet I've put myself to school,
And have learn'd (you see) to
    write
As fairly as I might.

The ladies were inclined
To be extremely kind;
And fain would me persuade
To quit my roving trade.
But my heart's a heart that
    wanders
Where the silver brook mean-
    ders.
My roof is the wide sky,
And a gipsy I must die.

Just now I've turn'd my skill
To good and not to ill;
And am helping Education
In this my own vocation.
Whate'er I gain to-day,
I mean to give away:
Tho' I fear me, as they say,
These British Schools will foil
My magic arts, and spoil
The people for believing,
And me, too, for deceiving.

Then come before this happens,
Lads and lasses, and be told,

What I could tell for silver,
But can better tell for gold.
Come! let me see the lines
By which palmistry divines;
On the tablet of your hands
How the dark future stands!
If the line of life be crost,
And in line of death be lost?
Where the line of fortune tends?
And the line of Venus ends?
Ah! long as maidens live,
They 'll be fools enough to give
Whatever they can spare
To know the shape and air
Of him who, ere my telling,
In their heart of hearts is dwell-
    ing.

Oh, silly, silly lassie!
If I told you, told you true;
You are thinking more of him
Than he ever thinks of you.
Nay! the truth I will not say,
For falsehood wins the day,
And no flattery—no pay!

I really should not spurn
Philosopher to turn;
But, as the world is made,
Mine own 's the better trade.

For Fortune, ancient queen,
Befriends my red cloak's sheen.
The Delphic tongues are dumb,
And she is hither come.
Yea, now she hath no shrine
But a sybil's eye—like mine.
Yet all men seek her still,
And so they ever will!
The wisest fain would learn
What next her wheel will turn.
And manhood's brow of pride,
That flings charms and spells
    aside,
Hath yet its " golden dreams,"
Hath yet its " magic schemes,"
More wild than most of mine,
In hieroglyphic line.

My wand is here to-day,
You have only now to say
That you fain would study more
Of my cabalistic lore.
There are many here around
Who can tell where I am found,
And will point with ready digit
To the cave of

        MOTHER BRIDGET.

1837.

LINES

WRITTEN THE MORNING AFTER QUEEN VICTORIA'S VISIT
TO THE CITY OF LONDON, NOV. 9, 1837.

'Tis o'er, and the grey morning dawns, as it dawneth
    every day,
The poetry and pageantry have in daylight died away;
The mighty mart of commerce wakes from a brief and
    brilliant dream,
Bequeathing it to history, as a meet and stirring theme.

Yes, history a tale will tell, of what yesterday hath seen,
All London up and out, to hail its young and radiant Queen;
From its mouldering tomb hath risen, the proud chivalry
    of old,
And display'd such scene before us as romance hath often
    told.

Though the temples and the towers in their shrouds of
    mist were wreathed,
With expectation's hum it seem'd, that each dome and
    turret breathed;
Whilst here and there, the cold grey stones, in their mas-
    sive contrast rose,
To the warm tints of moving life, and all its glittering
    shows.

The sun look'd down for one brief hour, as in joy on
    sight so fair,
The three estates of England's might, in concord meeting
    there ;
The Queen has pass'd confidingly, through her proud
    city's wards ;
No need of warriors round her, for her people were her
    guards.

How the dark war-horse paws in peace and gentleness
    the ground ;
Nor tramples on the wild glad throng, who so fearless
    stand around !
Whilst his rider's lance but flashes back, the glory and
    the glow
Of the scarlet and the silver, of the ebon and the snow.

They led thee to the banquet-hall, fair Lady of the isles,
Where gold and gems were lavish'd, to beseech thy gra-
    cious smiles ;
Soft light fell down on waving plumes, and on treasures
    of the mine ;
And Thou, the pearl amidst them all, did in peerless
    lustre shine.

Then fairies lit thy progress home, to the palace of thy sires,
Thy name was gleaming everywhere, in bright but harm-
    less fires ;
The solemn dome of old St. Paul's, in glistening splen-
    dours drest,
Had veil'd his own dim majesty, to greet his regal guest.

And ere that night thy crown'd head sought, the pillow
    of its rest,
How many thoughts, Victoria, must have stolen through
    thy breast!
In thy mother's arms a moment, was perchance fatigue
    beguiled,
As she whisper'd, " Thou hast found a home in Eng-
    land's heart, my child."

That mother's love hath fondly train'd, during youth thy
    docile will,
Trappings of state are round thee now, but she is near thee
    still ;
To warn, to guide, to comfort thee, in thy all too anx-
    ious way,
That early weight of care, I deem, she lifts it as she may.

And there is One, beloved Queen, thy God, and hers
    indeed,
Who has strength for all thy weakness, and wisdom for
    thy need ;
The welfare of these glorious realms, he has laid it in
    thine hand,
Entreat his guidance where to move, and entreat it where
    to stand.

Thy reign hath a bright beginning, and 'mid faction's strife
    and rage,
Fear not, thou art on the threshold of a fair millennial
    age ;

God grant thee grace and glory, as was thy sainted
    father's prayer,[1]
And to cast thy crown in Heaven before HIM who
    reigneth there !

---

[1] An interesting evidence of the Duke of Kent's devotional feelings is
recorded by a friend, who writes thus : "Two or three evenings previous
to his visit to Sidmouth, I was at Kensington Palace; and on my rising to
take leave, the Duke intimated his wish that I should see the infant princess in her crib; adding ' As it may be some time before we meet again,
I should like you to see the child, and give her your blessing.' The Duke
preceded me into the little princess's room, and on my closing a short
prayer that, as she grew in years she might grow in grace, and in favour
both with God and man, nothing could exceed the fervour and feeling
with which he responded in an emphatic Amen. Then with no slight emo-
tion he continued, ' Don't pray simply, that hers may be a brilliant career,
and exempt from those trials and struggles, which have pursued her father;
but pray that God's blessing may rest on her, that it may overshadow her,
and that in all her coming years she may be guided and guarded by
God."

NATURE HATH STORE.

NATURE hath store of ever new delights,
For him who seeks her with an earnest love;
Year after year, she bids such votary prove—
Whether he wanders o'er her mountain heights,
    Or treads her grassy vales—
    That she, thro' hills and dales,
Can sense of thrilling joy to him impart.
    And by each wilding spray
    Along a woodland way,
Hath power at will, to touch and charm his heart.
She wins him, if that heart be ill at ease,
To lay it open to the freshening breeze;
Scatters awhile its feverish thoughts in air,
And sends a sunbeam through its depths of care.

Oh, Nature is a calm, sufficing friend!
Yet nay!   She hath at will no change of mood,
No kindred feeling in her solitude,
That with the flow of restless life may blend.
    She hath nor hopes nor fears,
    Her very smiles and tears
Are passionless, nor own with ours a part;
    She smiles when we are sad,
    Oft weeps when we are glad.
The human heart still needs the human heart;

Much it receives of bliss from Nature's store,
Yet ever sues at friendship's shrine for more;
Sweet lore of woods and streams can read alone,
Yet longs for fellow-hearts to read its own.

Where we have linger'd with the friends we love
Do we not love to linger, yet again?
Albeit 'tis with a sense of soften'd pain;
As bright may heaven's arch be spread above,
  The earth as green and fair,
  We yet find missing there
The living soul, whence they their magic won!
  A tracery that was made
  Upon the landscape's shade,
By sunshine from affection's eyes is gone;
Yet still we linger—for amid such shade,
Rather than where that sunshine never play'd,
Low voices oft will fall on memory's ear,
And spirit-sympathies be hovering near.

There be some friends, the few, the far between,
Who have been changeless friends from youth to age;
Each chequer'd portion of our pilgrimage,
Their love has lighted, with its lamp serene;
  In sorrow's lonesome grot
  Where others sought us not,
They ever spoke sweet words of hope and cheer;
  And the dark hour pass'd by,
  In full content and joy;
Do we not seek them? love to have them near?

In absence unforgotten, life of life,
Spots of repose 'mid the world's fret and strife;
From time to time, we clasp their hands below,
And trust no separate bliss in heaven to know.

1854.

THE PEARL.

A MEDITATION ON THE SEA-SHORE.

Go, find a friend, and where, oh where,
Is found that "pearl" so pure and rare?
Not every shell, the waves of life
Cast in their lap of storm and strife,
Affords the gem to be enshrined
For ever in the constant mind.

Go, find a friend—that ocean wide
Has forms of beauty and of pride
At once to win th' admiring eye:
Yet not in these "the pearl" doth lie.
Its rougher bed, its homelier cell
Let the deep gulf of Ormus tell.

8

Go find a friend;—in early youth
We dream the dreams of trust and truth;
In every beauteous form we see
Look for the pearl confidingly;
Pursue—possess—and find there dwells
No treasure in the empty shells.

Go find a friend, He is not found
Always—where genius sheds around
Its dazzling phosphorescent light,
Like that which streaks the seas at night:
We may not trust that fitful ray
Alone to gild life's darkling way.

Go find a friend—dive deep—the pearl
Floats not on ocean's rippling curl.
Not every gleam from kindly eyes,
Where kindred feeling seeming lies
Must charm, till time and trial tell
If sorrow it can soothe as well.

Go find a friend, and first arise
To Him the " ark " doth symbolise;
A friend in Jesus—who can need
Aught other than the ' Friend indeed '?
His favour found—the " Pearl of price "—
Make life his willing sacrifice.

There may be hours of lonely pain,
Which earthly love would soothe in vain;
Nor life, nor death, have shades too deep
For Christ to watch the sufferer weep,

And gently dry each falling tear,
Saying, " Fear not! for I am here."

This Friend of friends, if thou hast tried,
For all thy need will still provide;
To him his hidden ones are known,
Through every land his pearls are strown;
Cast wheresoe'er thy lot shall be,
Some will find fellowship with thee.

And oh! when all these pearls are bound,
Those meek, once-suffering brows around,
Each fitting here, in several way
To crown him on that glorious day,
What matter how—what matter where—
So they at last are number'd there?

1838.

TO THE REV. JOHN WILLIAMS,

WITH AN ARTIST'S COLOUR-BOX AND SKETCHING FOLIO.

Ye rainbow tints, art's purest hues,
 How do ye win our souls away
From dusky cities, where they lose
 The power of Nature's green array!

Ye bring us dreams of sparkling rills,
    Of golden slopes and distance dim,
Of old beech woods, and rising hills,
    Bright pools the wild bird's wing doth skim,
Where oft, in many a lonely place,
The fair blue heaven reflects its face.

Go ye, but not to mock the light
    Of glitt'ring noon in English dales,
The sun that makes our moorlands bright,
    That same sun shines on far-off vales.
Go ye, where groves of corals rare
    Are branching in the clear deep seas;
Go where a hundred islets fair,
    May lovelier subjects yield than these;
Mirror the mountain's cloud-like shades,
And image Rarotonga's glades.

A hand your magic hues will spread
    Perchance while evening streaks the west,
Which beareth "life unto the dead,"
    From nobler toils awhile at rest:
That heart, each moment fain would seize
    Undying souls to seek and save,
And sound thro' all those southern seas,
    Tidings of worlds beyond the grave—
Parting from Albion's summits hoar,
For far Tahiti's palmy shore.

God speed the ship—the ship of peace!
    Let adverse winds in caverns sleep;

For her, may storm and tempest cease,
   And angels watch her o'er the deep.
At morn and even sacrifice,
   Through all our homes this prayer be pour'd,
That ocean's isles may now arise,
   And bring their tribute to the Lord;
Singing the night of darkness past,
Millennial morning dawns at last.

1838.

AUGUST.

WRITTEN IN A CORN-FIELD ON THE SEA-SHORE, AT HAVRE.

'TIS noon upon the waters,
   And harvest on the lea!
From the shadow of the sheaves
   Look out upon the sea!
Where the fishing-vessel glides
   White-wing'd unto its home;
And the far-off billow rides
   Each wave in silvery foam.

Faint blue is all the heaven,
   Fair green is all the sea;
The sleepy violet shadows,
   How beautiful they be!

The golden grain and shining sands
 Give back the sunny glow;
And for loveliness serener,
 Oh, whither would ye go?

This corn hath drunk the salt breeze
 Throughout the varying year,
The rushing tide hath murmur'd
 Oft to each waving ear.
'Tis ready for the garner,
 And this its song shall be,
'Tis noon upon the waters,
 And harvest on the lea!

1850.

OCTOBER.

OCTOBER's tints are golden,
 Howe'er her skies be grey:
A light no clouds can shadow,
 Attends her on her way.
The forest glows when she hath pass'd,
 And touch'd its verdant leaves,
As constantly stream'd o'er its head,
 The light of summer eves.

Like this, the peace residing
  In hearts by Heaven renew'd;
The gentle joys abiding,
  In souls to Christ subdued!
Though life were all with clouds o'ercast,
  Faith makes perpetual day;
The brightness earthly suns ne'er gave,
  They cannot take away.

1833.

NOVEMBER.

CHILL November! dim and drear,
Mourner of the waning year,
All the pomp of autumn shrouds,
In a veil of murky clouds.
He hath mutter'd to the deep,
And its waves in shadow sleep;
Long and low they touch the shore,
Cresting in their pride no more.
Who would court his sombre stay
In his robes of russet grey?
Like affliction come to cast,
Shade upon the sunshine past.

But, in summer hours serene,
'Mid the hues of pearl and green,
Would yon burning line of light
Linger, thus intensely bright,
Ocean's furthest verge to mark,
As now, that all beside is dark?
Hope in heaven—is like that ray,
In affliction's darkest day.

Hast thou mark'd the shadows glance,
O'er a landscape's wide expanse?
Playfully pursue the lights,
Scatter'd on the nearer heights;
Here in solemn depths conceal—
There in sunny breaks reveal,—
Spots—which owe their fairy power
To the magic of the hour.
Thus to me hath sorrow shown
Comfort else I ne'er had known;
Friendship's light more lovely made,
By affliction's circling shade.

1835.

TO THE OCEAN.

BLUE vault of waters, vast and deep,
　Wide as another sky;
How beautiful in noontide sleep,
　Thy giant billows lie!
Unruffled space, and awful rest,
In Heaven's broad cypher on thy breast.

Last night, thy loud and angry roar
　Answer'd each solemn cloud,
Sheet lightning to the trembling shore,
　Showing thee in thy shroud.
The starless skies above thee spread,
Black as thine own sepulchral bed.

What voice hath earth so old as thine
　Thou ever-sounding sea?
For worship nature owns no shrine
　So lone, so vast as thee,
Of Him who numbereth all thy waves,
And fathometh thy million graves.

That voice hath ne'er been hush'd in time
　Except, when thou wert spread
All silent, shoreless, and sublime,
　A world beneath thee—dead.
The ark—on gliding o'er thy gloom—
Sole epitaph on nature's tomb.

The earth hath lords; the peasant boasts
  Of mountains, as his own.
But the wide sea, O God of hosts!
  Belongs to Thee alone;
Nor man may print, nor time may trace,
Possession on its changeless face.

Yet once, the yielding ocean stood
  Firm, as an emerald floor,
As walls of crystal, it had form'd
  In ages gone before.
Jesus by night, the waters trod,
The yielding waters, own'd him God.

Twin-born of Time, a day shall be
  Of terror to the Earth,
When judgment-vials pour'd on Thee
  Shall herald its new birth,
The sea, like blood congeal'd, shall lie,
And all that dwell therein shall die.[1]

This sinful world by thy dark waves
  Once cleansed, and swept of old,
More fearful baptism yet must prove,
  In Holy Writ foretold.
Baptism of fire, for seas and skies,
Ere the " new earth" revealèd lies.[2]

---

[1] Rev. xvi. 3.   [2] 2 Pet. iii. 7.

Yet sure the glad millennial day
  Thy changèd face will see,
The glory! when the isles obey[1]
  The King of kings—O Sea!
And still beneath thy solemn waves,
Unrisen hosts will find their graves.

In after-time, with death and hell,[2]
  Thou shalt yield all thy dead;
And void before the great white throne,
  Shalt leave thy darksome bed.
The wicked thou must hide no more,
Thy saints, were render'd long before.[3]

There is a home where all shall meet,
  And none shall trouble them—
Whose place on earth was Jesus' feet,
  The New Jerusalem—
No sea, nor shore, O God, shall sever,
Thy ransom'd children then, for ever.

[1] Ps. lxxii. 8–10.   [2] Rev. xx. 13.   [3] Rev. xx. 5.

1841.

TO A YOUNG LADY ON THE DAY OF HER CONFIRMATION.

KNEELING among a sister train,
  Before no idol shrine,
Within an old and hallow'd fane,
  What thoughts to-day were Thine?
While the deep organ roll'd along
The vaulted aisle its holy song.

In simple robes of vestal white,
  Each like a youthful bride,
Hundreds around thee join'd the rite,
  And, bending side by side,
Confess'd their fathers' God was theirs,
And theirs the faith his word declares.

Ah! my Sophia—many there
  Who took that solemn vow,
Might only bow in seeming prayer,
  But not of these wert thou;
The light in thought, the vain in heart,
Oh not of these, I trust thou art.

The earthly shepherd's hand was laid
  On every suppliant near;
But Jesus knew what vows were paid
  By hearts in lowly fear;

And who besought his crook and rod
To guide them to the fold of God.

To such, whatever pilgrims need
 Was promisèd to-day;
No more on fruitless husks they feed
 In Zion's pleasant way;
Its living streams are pure and still,
And fair and green its holy hill.

As weary travellers retrace—
 When some high point they gain—
Their path, and every resting-place,
 Winding o'er steep and plain;
So thou shalt turn in life's decay,
And mark thy setting forth to-day.

Frowns of the world thou need'st not fear,
 But dread its syren smiles:
Go forth and prove thine armour here
 Against all Satan's wiles;
And when its links in death divide
May thy soul flee to Jesu's side.

1833.

A FAMILY PICTURE.

WE saw them rising, one by one,
  As years went fleeting by,
Saw each from infancy's soft night
  Ope childhood's laughing eye.
We saw them beat, with dancing feet,
  The greensward in their play,
When life was to their gladsome hearts,
  One long, fair, summer's day.

They swell'd into a numerous band,
  Methinks they number'd ten;
No shaft of death, nor fell disease,
  Had mission to them then:
God spared them to the anxious hopes
  Of those who loved them best;
Of those who now from hope or fear,
  For ever take their rest.

They grew together—sharing all
  That joy or woe might bring;
The fountain of their lives was fill'd
  From the same silver spring:
While here and there more closely twined
  One heart around another,
In that sweet love of early days,
  A sister's to a brother.

But years have fled, yes, many years,
    And it was Heaven's decree,
That that large household should divide,
    And every one go free:
Go singly free, to choose fresh homes,
    Forget their parting pain,
And ne'er beneath their old roof-tree
    Be bound as one again.

Since then the world's wide atmosphere
    Has cool'd their young regard—
New loves, new friendships, each has form'd,
    And each is bent to guard:
They dwell afar; and sympathies
    That gush'd in flowing tide
From all their hearts at once—alas!
    With time and change have died.

Offences come: If fortune smile
    And raiseth some on high,
Pride steppeth in, and humble friends
    Ambition passeth by.
If pinching poverty be known,
    Then every day hath cares,
And few the thoughts, from pressing want,
    The heart to others spares.

Ah! who can tell the thousand ways,
    By which disunion creeps,
Among the loved of former days,
    While old affection sleeps!

But two or three of all the ten
   Meet as they did of yore,
And some there are who scarce would reck
   If they should meet no more!

The father with his whiten'd hairs,
   The mother's eye of love,
In realms of bliss they do not see
   This scattering from above.
They drew all round them while they lived,
   They hush'd each petty ire,
And water cast on kindling sparks,
   Ere they could rise to fire.

Not thus should break life's dearest bonds,
   Not thus should union cease,
'Mid those who journey various ways
   To the same land of peace.
" Offences " in this sinful world
   " Must come," and be forgiven,
Or we ourselves no pardon ask
   From Him who dwells in heaven.

If angels made abode with us,
   All sinless, calm, and pure,
How would *they* meet the daily brunt
   That men from men endure?
With patience tireless as its need,
   With pardon, constant, mild,
And ne'er with bitter words would be,
   Him who reviled, reviled.

Enough—I never see a group
  Around their father's door,
But I think how time shall sever them
  When he shall be no more.
Each to their share of daily toil,
  Each to their load of care,
Which none of all their early mates,
  Perchance, shall know or share.

1842.

THE SONG OF THE CRYSTAL PALACE

IN HYDE PARK.

VICTORIA, pass thy Royal word—
  The word that rules the free;
Arrest the wild and ruthless work,
  Reverse the stern decree;
And let the Spirit of the Dome,
Nigh driven from its crystal home,
  Have audience of thee.

Give audience, Sovereign Lady,
  Daughter of Alfred's line;
Thy proudest Lords would not deny
  One high command of thine.

9

Give ear unto the Spirit-Queen,
Thou knowest all that she hath been
   And oftenest sought her shrine.

" Shall I flee from my shining halls,
   O Monarch of the Isles?
Shall they level my fairy walls,
   Where thousands met thy smiles?
Ah, surely, in thy inmost heart
My dazzling memories find a part,
   Dearer than nobler piles.

" I have shed to the winds my wealth;
   My gold and gems are gone;
And the more doth my peerless temple
   Abide in its beauty alone.
If that be to destruction hurl'd,
Which roof'd the riches of a world,
   'Tis stain upon thy throne.

" I have brought from fairyland
   What none e'er brought before;
I touch'd the millions with my wand
   As they pass'd my palace door;
And care, and want, and woe, and toil,
All dream'd a radiant dream awhile
   As they trod my sunlit floor.

" I bade the common work-day world,—
   The weary and the worn,
Itself enjoy the fruits it brings
   To men more nobly born.

Colour and form, in flower and gem,
I lavishly set forth for them,
   Too often held in scorn.

" And now, a hundred thousand tongues
   Shall speak the people's prayer,
That exiled I may never be
   From my realm so bright and fair.
High art, and poesy, and song,
But wait thy word to flock and throng,
   Into my kingdom there.

" 'Mid foliage of all genial climes,
   Children shall sit and tell,
What ne'er on all the earth beside
   Could be believed so well.
The sun shall stream with rainbow rays,
And moonlight flood with silvery haze,
   The spots where fountains fell."

Victoria, pass thy Royal word—
   The word that rules the free;
Arrest the wild and ruthless work,
   Reverse the stern decree;
And let the Spirit of the Dome,
Nigh driven from its crystal home,
   Find advocate in thee.

1851.

ON SELF-REGULATION.

" The faculty of self-regulation is more important to human happiness
and usefulness, than mere intellectual energy, or any surrounding
circumstances."

THERE are some people in this world who appear to make
no progress in moral existence; they pass their lives in labo-
riously doing nothing; they eat, drink, sleep, walk, visit,
dress, and at last—they die, apparently without exercising
any guidance over their own minds or those of others. If
isolated and single beings, they are often devoured with
ennui. If parents, they are followed to the grave, for the
most part, by a race like themselves.

There are others who having mental energy enough to
escape this dulness, yet possess such energy *unregulated;*
and perhaps this class is more actively mischievous than the
other. They allow mere circumstances to develop their
power; from among their ranks may come occasionally "a
great mind," that is, one eminent for the exhibition of some
peculiar faculty, and capable of intensity of useful pursuit—
possibly, a painter, an astronomer, a musician, a botanist, or
a geographer, adding to the stores of these various arts and
sciences, as much as the duration of their lives, and the
various gradations of their intellectual capacity may enable
them.

But fewer still, and rarely culled, even from this latter
division of society, are those, whether men or women, who

unite to intense power in pursuing their objects—that self-regulation which is the result of severe and habitual self-training, and which fits them consequently for the training of others. We will begin with tracing the culture of a well-regulated mind in infancy, and follow it through its various stages to maturity, as far as that word is applicable to any attainment in this imperfect world.

During the years of childhood we are regulated by others; and that mother best fulfils her duty who can soonest teach her child to begin to regulate itself. It seems that force of character is composed of three elements—physical energy, nervous energy, and mental energy; and that a man who possesses all three equally developed, and directed to worthy aims, has the power to be a very great man. Isaac Taylor, in his "Home Education," considers it as the duty of a mother to shelter the physical and nervous energy of her child during the first seven years of his life from over-tasking, that she may render him strong in these first two points for the successful culture of his mental energy at the commencement of the period of youth. If we look around us, even on those who are doing most in the world, we shall too often observe the workings of strong minds in weak bodies, and with shattered nerves; (such, alas! are most of our men of genius;) and, perhaps, if we could examine their early history, we might find that, gifted by God with the faculty of intense pursuit, they had wanted the above "shelter," and had been untrained to control and regulate the early movements of their minds. Precocious genius, power too early developed, and withdrawn from that repose and happy lack of notice which is its safest cradle, seldom lives to expand into its full strength, but passes from the earth, merely giving token of what it should and might have been.

But well-regulated infancy!—In order to secure this, there

must be inculcated early, by the means which seem most
fitted to the individual disposition, habits of obedience, patience, industry, and order—not the less important because
then exercised on trivial points.   For the sake of the physical energy, which will in health spontaneously show itself,
undue fatigue must be avoided, and for the nervous energy,
all extraordinary excitements shunned.   Especially must we
be careful not to foster vanity by display of any kind; for if
anything is beautiful in early days, it is simplicity and humility—so seldom seen, because so rarely cultivated.   The
sayings and doings of almost every little child are repeated
in its presence;—what should be the natural consequence,
but that it says and does things with the view to be observed?
Thus are nourished those early buddings of vanity and self-
conceit, which spring soon enough in an evil soil, without a
hot-bed to encourage them.   Those parents deal most wisely
with young children who can keep them the most humble—
their surest passport to the after-notice and favour of judicious friends.

. But to proceed to the regulation of youth.—We will now
suppose that there is constitutional vigour of body and nerve,
aided as much as possible by maternal care and nursery training, and that the child is prepared to enter on that course of
education which is to fit the man and the woman for their
places in society.

The first act of an instructor is to create a thirst for knowledge, and then to lead the mind, as it can bear it, into the
various paths of learning and science, as swiftly and easily as
all modern improvements may enable him.   But his second
aim must be to implant the habit of steady application; in
order to which, an inclination for particular studies, though
in some respects it should be considered—in others, must
not.   Those have made the finest characters in after-life who

have most fully understood the words—" *Must be done, whether you like it or not* "—in the days of their childhood; and
hence it is that even severe discipline, while it will make
three individuals out of four obstinate, shall so anneal the
mental force of the fourth, that he will be what he never
could have been without it.

The next following seven years of life, viz., from fourteen
to twenty-one, are, we think, the most important in fixing
the mould of future character; "and here," it was lately
observed to us by a judicious friend, who has proved emi-
nently successful in the training of a family, " occurs a difficult point for the governor, and a most critical one for those
governed."

The eye of the mind, we will suppose, is opened, the
powers half developed, the judgment immature, and the
desire for independence born. From this point many, and
indeed, most young people start off on the road of their own
devices, whatever that may be. They like and tolerate—for
we will not desecrate the words "love and honour"—their
parents in proportion as they permit them to do as they
please; and as soon as possible, prudently or imprudently,
are bent on settling in the world for themselves. These,
however, are *not* well-regulated minds. "It is good for a
man that he bear the yoke in his youth," says Jeremiah;
and this assertion may be especially applied to these seven
years. A curb and a check, however distasteful, are at this
period necessary; and in the minds of those who remain
under their parents' roof, its influence should be aided by a
conviction of its importance. These are the years in which
the art of self-regulation is to be studied by the young, and
the science of self-government diligently practised, without
which they will never become fit in their turn to govern
others. Those among them make the best heads of houses

who unite to natural decision and firmness, the uniform dignity of self-control, which is a habit scarcely to be acquired but in youth, and while under the authority and dominion of others. Many parents, finding it difficult to hold the rein over adolescence, are weak or indolent enough to drop it; but woe to the family where this is the case! No dominion is without its difficulties, domestic or national, and power must reside somewhere: is it to be with the head or with the members of a body? If true piety reigns in the ruling mind, and is happily transmitted to those ruled, the wheels of government should move easily and cheerfully along. But we must not wait for perfection in the governing party before we sustain and submit to its power. The pride of equality and the love of competition, too commonly shown by young people towards their elders and superiors, can be effectually repressed by nothing short of their own conviction of its impropriety, which will induce a patient waiting for the time when others shall gradually depend on them for direction, and when they shall afford what they at present receive.

The art of self-regulation includes attention to the claims of method and order, a foresight of plan and purpose, so that one duty or pursuit shall not intrench upon the season due to another; and the non-observation of this, so very frequently renders men of genius so little domesticated, or desirable as companions in private life,—their intensity of pursuit carrying them forward through continuous days and successive nights, to the ultimate destruction of their nervous energy, and the overtasking of their physical power, regardless meanwhile of all minor moralities; in which eccentricity they too often glory, and say, their "attention will not bear distracting a moment from their object till it is attained." Had the habit, however, been formed in early life, is it not probable that their mental power would have proved the

fresher for their purpose, from its due relaxation and recon-
centration?

Another article of self-regulation lies in the right subser-
viency of mental power to moral excellence. This is especially needed in women, who will hereafter become, in their
own houses, the springs of propriety, good feeling, and order;
and must give tone and temper to the atmosphere of their
families. How important that their own personal actions
should be all upon principle! Men may think that they do
good by appearing to storm and to drive; but the province of
a wise woman is herself fixedly to proceed in the path of
duty, and to expect that those she leads will follow. A passive
and negligent mistress is no blessing to a household; but
mental energy, in its mere possession, is not enough to
woman;—she must have balance of character—at least an
equal proportion of moral sense to the quantum of her intellectual faculty. Wordsworth has drawn her portrait:—

> " Yes, she must be, with eye serene,
>   The very pulse of the machine—
>   A being, breathing thoughtful breath,
>   A traveller betwixt life and death.
>   The reason firm, the temperate will,
>   Endurance, foresight, strength, and skill;
>   A perfect woman, nobly plann'd
>   To warn, to comfort, and command;
>   And yet, a spirit still, and bright,
>   With something of an angel light."

Self-regulation is peculiarly shown by the way in which
mothers can meet life's difficulties, trials, and small daily
thwartings. If we do so calmly and patiently, we rise above
them. If they fret us, and despoil us of our inward comfort,
we have not yet made the use which God intends we should
make of them; for, whatever they may be, they are *His* school

for our tempers; and to the lesson He has seen fit for us to learn, we had better apply as sedulously as we can. It is not good, even for the wisest and the best of human creatures, to be entirely uncrossed and without contradiction. Christ, although perfect, endured the "contradiction of sinners against himself," thereby leaving us an example to endure likewise.

We have only one farther remark to make, viz., that self-regulation is a voluntary and a personal thing. People cannot be forced into it, though they may be trained towards it; and perhaps we only feel its full importance when we are left to the pressure of our own responsibility. It is not necessary to do any more than refer to the standard of Scripture, that index, by the study of which, the work can only effectually proceed. Such is the manual, and such ought those who adopt it to become. When will those who have professed Christianity be so watchful in their conduct as to leave no room for those who reject it—to say, "I see nothing in these people to prove that they *are* as they declare—the disciples of Jesus?" "Let him that is without sin in this matter cast at his brother the first stone."

1848.

LLYN CYNFAL,

FESTINIOG, NORTH WALES.

WHEN the red thunder-cloud bursts on Moel-Wyn,
Speed to Llyn Cynfal, nor heed for the rain;
If a glimpse of the Fall thy courage shall win,
Thou'lt see it, as ne'er thou might'st see it again.
The storm and the twilight are fittest array
For the torrent that swept the young Maiden away;
Far fitter than glittering sunshine and day.

From yon rocky pulpit, the spirits of air,
'Mid the thunder's groan and the lightning's glare,
Fling the glowing flood to the pools beneath,
Down deep to those terrible chambers of death,
Where none heard the last sigh, or caught the last prayer
Of the agonized being, precipitate there!
Heed thy steps! thou art treading the same mossy stair.

She left in the morning, light-hearted, the inn,
To seek, with her brothers, the perilous Llyn;
One slip, in one moment, and lost to the eye,—
Dash'd forth by the waters, white garments rush by.
O'er each sharp rifted crag the poor corse roll'd in doom,
Till borne back to the door which she left in her bloom,
And folded in grief for the sorrowful tomb.

1853.

GRIEF.

" Sleep, that knits up the ravell'd sleave of care.
The death of each day's life, sore labour's bath,
Balm of hurt minds."—*Macbeth*.

YES, mighty Master, sleep shall still
　" Knit up care's ravell'd sleave,"
And rest, too, in her ebon realms,
　Shall weary ones receive.

And still through all the quiet land,
　The same soft waters stray,
To lave the pain of aching limbs
　A little while away.

But tell me not that sleep hath power,
　Or cure, or rest, or calm
For the heart's wounds—that it should turn
　Their bitterness to balm.

When all deep feeling's chords have been
　To last endurance strung,
Till there might never further sound
　From the spent lyre be wrung;

Around such couch dark visions wait,
　Which may sleep's minions seem
To whisper to the miserable,
　That misery is a dream.

They may lift sorrow's ponderous load,
  One moment from the soul;—
'Tis but to edge its agony,
  And not to make it whole.

They rend the gall a little while
  From memory's bitter store;
They 'll cast it back into the heart,
  More bitter than before.

No! woe had rather watch and weep,
  While nightly vigils steal;
Than sleep to think the past a dream,
  And wake its truth to feel.

Then tell me not that sleep hath power,
  Or cure, or rest, or calm
For the heart's wounds—that it should turn
  Their bitterness to balm.

THE DOWNS, BRIGHTON,

INSCRIBED TO A LADY WHO USUALLY WENT BY THE NAME OF
" ST. MARY."

WHERE are the sweet St. Mary's thoughts?
  With the scene before her?
Are they of the calm blue sky,
  The blue sky shining o'er her?
Scarce a cloud across it streams,
  And the sun at noon,
Mocks at Midsummer—and beams
  In April as in June.

Hath she sent them far and wide,
  With those fairy sails?
Sprinkled o'er the ocean-tide,
  By the sportive gales?
Else were the sea another sky;
  For not a wave's white crest
Upon the silvery surface breaks,
  The beauty of its rest.

We're sitting on a green hill-side,
  And hills around us be;
Between whose swelling outline flows
  That bright and silver sea!

'Mid prickly beds besprent with bloom,
  The gowan's golden store,
For us, and for the honey-bees,
  To reckon o'er and o'er.

The noise of waves upon the beach,
  The town's far distant hum;
If e'er these airy heights they reach,
  As wandering sounds must come.
But for the speech of passer-by,
  Or laugh of joyous child,
The lark alone is heard on high,
  Trilling his matins wild.

Now where are sweet St. Mary's thoughts?
  I deem the landscape's rest,
The sunshine of this happy hour
  Pervades her gentle breast;
For e'en if aught of care or pain,
  The past or future crost,
Its influence for awhile were vain,
  And in the present lost.

Not often 'mid the city's strife,
  But on the green hill-side,
Did Jesus speak the words of life
  To those for whom he died.
And still they seek to muse his love
  Such intervals of peace—
An earnest of that heaven above,
  Where strife for aye shall cease.

1835.

ADDRESS TO A FRIEND,

ON FIRST HEARING A SOSTENENTE PIANO-FORTE * PLAYED BY ITS
INVENTOR, A GREAT MUSICAL GENIUS.

DORA! 'tis o'er; those rich low tones
    Retiring, were the last;
The strain has died in the halls of pride,
And the spell, like all things bright beside,
    With the passing hour is past.
    Devotion's trancing swells,
    The distant vesper-bells,
    All melody and might,
    Lost in the quiet night.

'Tis o'er; yet oft this strain will steal
    Upon our evening dreams.
Arise and away, with dawning day,
Again on life's dusty, beaten way.
    But music haunts twilight streams;
    And sleep's dim land hath heard,
    Warbled as by a bird,
    Each thrilling tone anew,
    And memory own'd it true.

* The effect of this instrument is magical. By the use of different
pedals, it imitates every other to perfection—trumpet, bugle, flute, harp,
organ, Æolian harp, etc.

For music stood reveal'd that hour,
    Its science and its soul ;
In cadence strong, with the voice of song,
How the chords of glory roll'd along !
      Till forth each feeling stole—
      On " trumpet" blast upborne,
      Roused by the " bugle-horn ;"
      Eager to rally round,
      Th' inspiring tide of sound.

The wind is abroad—ah ! we know
    Whence that sigh Æolian came.
We heard the swell, and we feel the spell,
But never may gaze on the viewless shell ;
      Th' enchanter sits the same.
      Yet the wind's spirit-wings
      Have rush'd across the strings :
      And we wept until at length
      The sweetness swell'd to strength.

The music of the spheres hath pass'd ;
    Mingle sweet flute and lyre ;
Unseen ye came, yet we know ye came,
Tho' still th' enchanter sits the same.
      Did ages past aspire,
      By pipes of varied kind,
      To sway th' immortal mind?
      This hath the triumph won,
      To blend their tones in one !

1837.

Beseeching thy bright pencil; but this brow,
This eminence of all, rewards delay
With subjects fairest. We had climb'd the heights
Which in their robe of woods shut in our vale,
Whose highest trees are our horizon line.
Behind their delicate fringe the streaks of dawn
First redden, and the rainbows touch the ground.
A few steps onward, and wide vales beyond
Would now rise emulous on our ravish'd sight;
So beauty waits us here on every side.

That far-off city, empress of the earth,
Lends a proud lustre to this sylvan hill.
Her abbey, palaces, and spires, all break,
Like beautiful pictures, on its solitude,
Sometimes defined, and sometimes indistinct,
Like buildings in a dream.   The pencil chose
A point where summits soften'd into clouds,
Seem'd like blue sea, and plains by sunbeams lit,
Were as a lake's calm floor, reflecting heaven,
With mimic islets, and soft shady shores;
Such distance well contrasted foreground bold
And broken; underwood and wilding spray,
And sparkling gem, full worth such careful setting,
The one bright birchen Tree.
                              I will not grieve
To think this precious gift, this perfect skill
To take possession of fair forms, and fix
Rich tints before they fade, was never mine;
This scene, to thee a new delight—for years
Has had its living likeness in my heart,

Making sweet summer there.

      Those dark green woods
Were ever spread before my childhood's eye,
And first I loved them as a child, because
I saw them always from my father's door;
And then I loved them with a new wild love,
As link'd with youth's romance of varied hours;
Its radiant joys and sorrows, fancied real,
Had mystical relation to these shades;
They read me the first lines of poesy
In nature; and they were the first still forms
Invested with that bright ideal beauty
Which yet is more than mere reality.

 And now in riper years, when earth is found
To be a wilderness, with all its charms,
Seeking for rest, my spirit often pines
To leave awhile the trifling, vexing crowd—
When it is ruffled into feverish heat;
When it is stirr'd, and its smooth surface crost
By change and care, I suffer it to seek
The calm society of woods and streams;
Their gentle whispers oft restore content,
And hush repining.   They are quiet friends,
Who never vex full hearts with idle questions,
But look in silence back their own sweet smile,
And teach their own serene tranquillity
To wounded spirits.

     God hath given rest
Unto the human hearts which He hath made,
Thro' silent influence of his outward works.

Well may I love to look upon this page
Of nature's book. Well may I fear to trust
The feelings which it wakes unto cold words,
Lest Poetry, which here in silence breathes,
In utterance should depart.

1833.

THE COMMON TREASURE.

AN ALLEGORY.

WE were lately in company with an individual, who, being thrown into the mesmeric sleep, was discovered to possess the faculty of clairvoyance; and, during the time it continued, he made some singular disclosures, of which we have transcribed notes for the benefit of our readers.

Each member of the community, taking the hand of the mesmeriser, was in his turn " put into communication" with the mesmerised; and as the countenance of the latter expressed much wonder, he was asked what occasioned it. " I see," said he, " in the midst of you a great heap of treasure, which is neither gold, nor silver, nor precious stones, but still immensely valuable! It is to be divided amongst you; and though you will each be entitled to an equal quantity of it, to be daily received, you will comparatively make so different a use of your several portions, that it is at the results which I foresee, that I am so amazed."

The company were then all presented to him in their turns.
They were a very mixed company; and the first person
whose condition he investigated was a Day-labourer, earning
half-a-crown a-day for the maintenance of himself and
family. The examiner seemed satisfied with him as a speci-
men of the class he represented. "Your treasure is well
spent in your degree," said he; " you realize with it a sufficient portion of the necessaries of life; and by each day's effort
you are strengthening the muscular power which your vocation
requires. If you improve your mind with the small remnant
of your capital, that, too, will be strengthened fourfold; you
will rise to a superior condition of your calling, and obtain
better wages. There is a great variety in day-labourers—
some are born to wheel a barrow and shoulder a hod, from
the cradle to the grave; you are not exactly one of these,
though even they may be praiseworthy in their way: you
have a wish to rise; and if the wish gives place to steady
effort, you will succeed in your endeavour."

The next person who appeared before the clairvoyant was
an Artificer, another member of the working-classes; but in a
position where skill, as well as early training, had been necessary to evolve the power required in his profession. "You,"
said the speaker, " have great pleasure in the manual dex-
terity which you have gained by practice, and in that successful and successive repetition of efforts which constitutes your
talent. True it is that the curse annexed to labour is sweet-
ened; for the calling forth of faculty of any kind gives satis-
faction to the employed, independently of the pleasure of its
earnings and its wages." He, too, was pronounced to be
turning his treasure to account.

The third person who came under inspection was a Dan-
seuse; and she had, besides the talent of amusing a certain
portion of the public, the art of turning her treasure into a

great heap of gold—but it was not without vast effort. She had expended a life on the mere education of her toes, so as to pirouette upon these extremities as other people cannot do. She had undergone, daily from her childhood, what she herself called torture, and the most exhausting fatigue; so that after the morning lesson which was to prepare her for the night's exhibition, she often fell fainting on the floor of her chamber; and the agility and marvellous bounds of the evening, the seeming floating on the air, were only to be obtained at a price like this; yet her end, such as it was, was abundantly answered. She cleared hundreds of pounds by a single performance; and more money in a season than men of science often obtain, for a lifetime spent in the most valuable services to mankind.

A young Lady was the next who glided forward to take her portion of the treasure. "And you," said the sage sleeper, " will pride yourself in having it all upon your hands; for in England there is a sort of elevation annexed to leisure, to the state of not being obliged to work, and of not being obliged to do anything well enough to gain by it, which is unfortunately a premium to mediocrity."

This young lady did not exactly spend her treasure—a great deal of it slipped from her fingers, she knew not how. An artist who looked at her drawings, pronounced them " passable for a lady;"—a musician said the same of her singing. Further she did not much trouble herself; for dressing and visiting, and a modicum of useless fancy-work, filled up the rest of her time. She was waiting in hopes of an advantageous settlement in life; and yet the clairvoyant could not pronounce that she was particularly cognizant of duty towards those to whom she at present stood most nearly related, or that she was employing her treasure in any way, to purchase what might be useful to her when she should be married—yet there was nothing that that treasure would not have purchased; and she might rationally expect to enjoy a much less portion of it when she changed her condition.

Her Brother's portrait was a tolerable pendant to her own. The clear-sighted visioner was able to undress people's character to themselves without giving offence, as he was totally unconscious, on awaking, of all that he had said to them. Like his sister, it happened that this youth's portion of the treasure was at his own disposal. He did not necessarily belong to the working-classes. As a boy at school, he had been remarkable for merriment and mischief, and particularly for inapplicancy. He had not, as a child or as a youth, acquired any one thing thoroughly; therefore he had, in after years, what Carlyle calls, no "can do" in him. He had read, during his existence, thousands of newspapers and reviews. He had played hundreds of games at chess. He was very well able to amuse himself; and many years' income of his treasure were gone: yet, on arriving at full manhood, he had but little to show for it. If he aimed at a worthy object, he presently changed it. A little difficulty daunted him, and interruption put him out of temper. He loved not labour, and he was not obliged to undertake it. Indeed, in middle age, he had scarcely the power to do so. The clairvoyant only remarked to him, "I should think it would have been a mercy for you if you had been early obliged to turn your treasure into bread. Now, scarcely less than the perseverance of a Demosthenes would enable you to do so."

In bright contrast to these young spendthrifts came a Mother, whose heart was filled with a deep sense of the value of "the common treasure," and at whose disposal stood not only her own portion of it, but the direction of that which belonged to the various members of her household. As her little ones in turn awoke from the soft, sweet night of infancy,

and she saw each active intelligence rising by degrees above
the toys and trifles of the nursery, saying, " I shall be happy
when I have always something to do," she caught gladly at
the desire, and thoughtfully and judiciously supplied the
need. She thought it as much her duty to do this as to
provide for them their food or raiment; and she went
further—she trained them in after years to spend their treasure wisely for themselves; and her children " arose up to
call her blessed." From their happy home they went forth
rich in mental resources, and rich in energy to make any
home happy. They knew no dull and vacant hours; the
solitude of country retirement was never wearisome to them;
the lounge of the morning call, the gossiping repetition of
immaterial and trifling facts, often added unto by most mischievous fictions, seemed to them an invasion of their valuable
inheritance; and while they sought, at fitting seasons, the
invigorating society of the wise and good, they had one perpetual aim, after their mother's example, to preserve their
treasure from being frittered away, and to dedicate it in
valuable portions to some noble and worthy end. There was
one son of that mother who rewarded all her care, and who
stood forth with a thoughtful and impressive brow, a speaking
eye, and a mind which " dealt with all philosophy," by whom
the treasure was spent in high pursuit of knowledge and
pure science,—and not only in pursuit, but in attainment.
He precisely knew what other men had done in his vocation;
and he added his brand to the undying flame which they had
kindled. " You are using your treasure, sir," said the seer—
and, at the same time, such a light passed over his countenance, that he was again asked what he saw. " I am standing," said he, " on the shore of a dark stream; and now I
have taken a new view of your heap of treasure. I told you
it was not gold nor gems, but that it was very precious; and

so it has been, as you may have employed it earnestly or negligently in acquiring the good you might require on earth; but now I see that it is priceless, priceless! for another end. Oh, woe to those who have wasted it! God gives it in equal portions to the meanest and the highest, mainly to prepare them for fording this dark stream. He will bring man to Eternity; and He gives him as its preface—Time. Time is given him to gain his bread by the sweat of his brow, or of his brain; and to give to those whom he gathers round him in a household, the food, the clothing, the education, and the position in society which they have a right to expect from him; but from these lawful aims he must take leisure to prepare himself and them for eternity."

Those only in this company are using their treasure as nobly as it may be used, who are daily and devotionally drawing nearer to their Saviour, and seeking always to multiply the willing subjects of His realm; to arouse the sleeping, to give sight to the blind, hearing to the deaf, and understanding to the simple. These only are, in the eye of Heaven, the working classes; and angels respect not those who can live content without this labour.

1849.

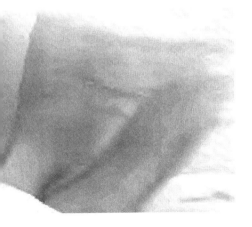

THE OLD HOME.

ON LEAVING * * * * * * *, AFTER A RESIDENCE OF MANY YEARS.

CAN any kindred band depart,
Unheeding, from their place of rest,
When years have made the shelter'd nest
    Warm to the heart?
Albeit another home be found—
Will not the hearth once circled round
    Still live in memory's chart?
For love, like Ivy, oftenest twines
In freshness, o'er forsaken shrines.

The home where human hearts have shared
Succeeding scenes of joy and care,
Ah! silent things have voices there!
    It oft hath fared
That quiet forms in after years,
Have haply touch'd those hearts to tears;
    And they have felt and cared
For a remember'd flower or tree,
    With an old friendship's sympathy.

Yes! some can ne'er forget that here
First-love was nursed of bud and bell,
And first in nature found a spell,
    Which, year by year,
Has strèngthen'd in the enthusiast soul
Its power to brighten and console;
    In grief to soothe and cheer,
And crown the cup which pleasure brings,
With sparkling drops from purest springs.

And set apart in this dear home,
Some spots are sacred to the past,
Where those we loved were look'd on last;
    Those who shall come
No more our glad embrace to meet;
Whom other thresholds ne'er shall greet,
    From out the quiet tomb.
Their spirits haunt this tranquil scene,
We go—where they have never been.

Friendship hath made, amid these bowers,
Its sweetest music to our ears;
Kindled our hopes and hush'd our fears,
    In by-gone hours.
More fondly still, remembrance broods
Over those cherish'd solitudes,
    Which will no more be ours.
And oh! it hallows all the ground,
If here the Pearl of price was found.

Where melted first the heart of stone,
Where first was sought the ear of Heaven;
Where peace was felt, and sin forgiven
　　By blood alone.
The soul subdued must gladly raise
Its lowly hymn of grateful praise;
　　And ever love to own
How fire by night, and cloud by day,
Have guided since its onward way.

The fire upon our altar dies!
The traveller's staff is in our hand,
And girded to depart, we stand.
　　Oh, let there rise
Incense of praise for mercies past,
In columns fragrant to the last.
　　Our hidden future lies
Safe with a Father and a Friend,
Who ne'er shall change till time shall end.

And will that Father still bestow
His blessing when our hearts are glad,
His comfort when those hearts are sad,
　　Where'er we go?
Then calmly forward may we press,
Nor fear to meet the bitterness
　　Of any lot below.
In hope that we at last shall rise
To homes enduring in the skies.

1832.

TO A BROTHER,

ON HIS FIFTEENTH BIRTH-DAY.

THE world before Thee lies—
  Thy childhood's dreams are o'er ;
Life, like a sunlit sea at morn,
  Tempts thee to leave the shore.
Thy little bark is trimm'd with care,
A mother's love, a father's prayer,
  The favouring gale implore ;
And crave that Heaven will kindly guide
Their treasure o'er the treacherous tide !

Hope lightens o'er thy brow,
  Joy dances in thine eyes,
Nor cloud nor shadow markest thou
  Along th' horizon rise.
Ah! who would dim youth's glance of fire?
Ah! who would damp its high desire?
  Yet every wave that dies
Upon the shore, in silver spray,
Has made some bark like thine its prey.

This—time erewhile shall teach,
  Life will not pass away,

And leave the rose-lights of thy lot
  Fresh as they are to-day ;
As yet, the world is bright and strange ;
When it is full of care and change,
  Then turn thee back, and lay
Thine hopes and fears alike to rest,
Upon the hearts that love thee best.

How did a sister hail
  Each kindling of the soul,
When late thy spirit woke to thought,
  And aim'd at its control.
I would not that the cares of time
Should quench that sympathy sublime,
  And Mammon o'er it roll,
To whelm in current, dark and cold,
The light of mind in love of gold.

Yet, if I pray'd to read
  The folded roll of fate,
It would not be with pride to mark
  Thee noble, rich, or great:
Nor should I hope to read thy name
Enshrined upon the page of fame,
  But pass to Heaven's gate,
And gaze into its temple fair,
To see if thou hadst enter'd there !

Beloved !—wouldst thou choose
  A guide unto that land,
Whose voice the winds and sea obey ?
  Behold Him, waiting, stand :

It cannot be that blush of shame
Crimsons thy cheek to own His name.
  Oh! clasp His pierced hand,
Then part in peace!   Such aid divine
Be evermore to thee and thine.

1831.

TO A SISTER.

" For wonder faine I wolde her see,
  So mokle it enchanted me,
  That when I saw her on a morrow,
  I was warished of all my sorrow;
  Of all day after, till 'twere eve,
  Methoughten nothinge might me grieve."—*Chaucer.*

SOME grace of outward form or mien
  Thus waked the harp of elder time;
'Tis crumbled long to dust, I ween,
  And lives but in this deathless rhyme.
The chisell'd lip, the vermeil cheek,
  The liquid eyes, whose lustrous fire,
Could once beyond expression speak,
  Have sated now the worm's desire.

But, oh, my Sister, yester-eve,
  That poet's lyre was strung for me;

' Methoughten nothinge might me grieve,'
   Since yester-eve I look'd on Thee.
It was no charm of face or mien,
   That waked a joy which angels share;
I look'd upon a soul serene,
   Escapèd from the fowler's snare.

Like a young bird encaged and bound,
   It late had struggled to be free,
But Satan clasp'd its fetters round,
   Till Jesus whisper'd, ' Come to me!'
And now it seeks His lighter yoke,
   Its wings are fain to soar above,
The spells of pride and doubt He broke,
   For He is power, and He is love.

The ancient master of the lyre
   Had long'd his queenly fair to see,
But ne'er so fervent his desire
   As ours, for day like this to thee.
There's one in heaven, my precious child,
   Who early left a world of sin,
Oh, how that brother would have smiled,
   To mark thy Christian course begin!

Thou scarce his image may'st retain,
   Thou knewest not his soft, dark eye,
Playing beside his couch of pain,
   In curly-headed infancy!

11

" *His* baby," oft he named thee, ere
   God call'd him to his heavenly home ;
And he will welcome thee, whene'er
   Thou also to that rest shall come.

There's one in heaven, and more on earth,
   Who in thy joy shall now rejoice ;
This season of thy second birth,
   Arrives in answer to the voice
Of prayer, gone up at eventide;
   A father oft hath pray'd such prayer,—
Nor is a mother's hope denied,
   And I would claim a sister's share.

Another joins our pilgrim band,
   Another heart is set on high ;
Another drawn by grace to stand,
   Apart from earthly vanity !
Another owns the Pearl of price,
   The balm for all life's various ill ;
The light, that leads to Paradise,
   The good, which the void heart can fill.

Yes ! ' they shall find, who early seek !'
   Now launch thee on time's rapid stream,
Young voyager ! thy strength is weak,
   And rough and dark the waves may seem ;
Thyself the helm thou must not guide,
   But place it in thy Saviour's hand.
In storm or tempest he shall hide,
   And safe on heaven's blest shore shall land.

Tears tremble in thy soften'd eye,
  Wounded for sin, thy spirit feels,
The tears that Jesus loves to dry,
  The wounds that Jesus gladly heals.
Seek him in silence day by day,
  Go—softly walk in faith and prayer,
Lead others in the narrow way;
  May all thy kindred meet thee there!

1837.

TO

MY MOTHER ON HER BIRTHDAY.

My Mother! thy name is a sacred name,
  It hath e'er been precious in former years;
But it never fell with so sweet a claim
  On my ear, so moving my heart to tears,
As it does in this year, whose dawn hath smiled
On the sunny brow of our *own* dear child.

For his little life is an open page,
  Where I read the debt which to thee is due;
How countless and nameless, the tender cares,
  Which thou hast forgotten, and I scarce knew!
Can I feel the love which he needs from me,
And not turn to the past, and think on thee?

'Tis sweet to trace to its earliest birth,
   That beautiful feeling which never dies,
The strongest and deepest affection on earth
   Is the mother's love of self-sacrifice!
Hard were the heart that could coldly repay
Such devoted love at a later day.

No! it never dies!—In this year beside,
   What had nigh been the couch of death to me,
Thou hast tireless stood, e'en when danger tried,
   And watching had wearied all else but thee:
I felt in thy step, and heard in thy tone,
The comfort that comes, from a mother alone.

Thou hast touch'd the brow of the hill of time,
   Thou hast set thy face to the vale of years:
And for me, who have yet that steep to climb,
   And to meet the hosts of its hopes and fears,
How oft thou'rt seeking to smooth the way,
And warn of thy slips in a former day!

As the upward path, I am toiling along,
   In this world where joy without care is not—
Weeping sometimes—but oft too with a song
   Of praise to Him who so mingles our lot:
May God grant me grace, to my child to be
The friend that my Mother has been to me!

The burden and heat of the day have worn
   Thy once gay spirits to sober tone;

May those thou hast nurtured in youth and strength
   Never leave thee now to thy load alone:
'Twere bliss, if to thee I one pain could spare,
Or soften one sorrow, or lighten one care.

In turning the Books of the Future and Past,
   Should thine eye not rest on their brightest page—
Be it mine to point thee where sunlight is cast,
   Away from earth's shadows, thy soul to engage:
Beyond and above the small troubles of time,
May love lead us together, in flight sublime.

There's a world to which, in the days of old,
   Thou hast often guided my childhood's eye;
Let us gaze from afar on its gates of gold,
   By the glass of faith bring it daily nigh:
And, oh, in that world, ever side by side,
My Mother, may thou and thy child abide!

1840.

TO THE SAME,

A FEW YEARS LATER.

MY Mother,—summer suns once more
Dapple with light the grassy floor,
Of our fair valley—Thou and I,
Still dwell there, as in days gone by;
Content and glad, whate'er betide,
That there we sojourn side by side.

And five swift rolling years have fled
Since last I think, I sang or said,
How mother's love in heart of mine,
More closely bound my heart to thine.
What further can I sing or say,
But this, with added love, to-day?

Time, Change, and Death, those mighty powers,
For ever on earth's fairest bowers,
Inscribing 'Ichabod '—have riven
From us no gift that God had given;
And yet he multiplies the store,
Oh! for glad hearts to praise him more.

In years to come, how fondly back
Will memory scan life's present track;

These summer-eves, so bright and still,
These sunsets fair, o'er stream and hill;
These waving trees, those brilliant flowers;
This rich repose, so fully ours!

Nor sooner shall reflection tire,
Of thoughts on the glad winter fire;
The blazing logs that flash'd on tiles,
Like the large hearths of Gothic piles;
And the wide circle meeting there,
Eve's pleasant converse closed with prayer.

We dare not dream on aught which may
Break up this band in future day;
Yet who can look for changeless ties,
And deem for them no louring skies
Can darken, on this sinful earth,
Now travailing for nobler birth?—

Therefore, my Mother, I would bring
As love's small-token offering,
A picture of the glorious morn,[1]
That on the saints of God shall dawn—
Dawn amid judgments fierce and deep,
On those who in their sins shall sleep.

Here, oftentimes our hopes of joy
Meet in fruition such alloy,

[1] "The Silver Trumpet," by Rev. O. Winslow.

A cloud so dark, with sullen dye,
Can gloom athwart the purest sky;
That earth's most shelter'd vales within,
We own the power of woe and sin.

But yet, in prophecy, appears
A day—"As of a thousand years";
A day remaining to the Lord,
And clearly imaged in his word,
When Christ upon the earth shall reign,
And Satan's raging power restrain.

More of his "glory" to believe,
More of his wisdom to receive;
With Him—and with his saints to be,
In that long day of Jubilee
Gather'd—with all we love, be Thine;
And oh! my Mother, be it mine!

1845.

TO A BROTHER

ON HIS COMING OF AGE.

WHAT garland, dear one, shall I weave for thee
On this thy natal day?   No skill is mine
To twine for thy young brows a classic wreath,
(The Grecian laurel, springs not in our vale).
Small clustering cares and joys, of household kind,
Do now oft fetter too, my woman's heart,
From roving as it did in times of old;
But yet the sight of thee, and erst the sound
Of thy fraternal lyre, have touch'd the strings
Of mine, long silent; and it must pour forth
A few fond notes of welcome and of love.

My brother, thine has been a thoughtful youth—
A youth of deeper thought than most men's age—
And still, with all thy philosophic lore
Thou hast a poet's heart.   A sympathy
With all things beautiful, a happy power
To cull from nature and from common life
Ethereal essence, and to shed it back,
Into congenial souls—the poet's crown
Were yet, I deem, too low an aim for thee.
Thou hast forsaken the paternal hearth
The din of traffic, and the paths of gain,
For holier things than these—that thou may'st prove

'Wise to win souls' from the wide realms of sin.
We touch on solemn times—division, change,
Disruption—mark the world's advancing age,
And I oft ponder on thy destiny
Amidst it all, young aspirant, with prayer
That God, who hath bestow'd rich gifts of mind,
And turn'd that mind toward himself, may keep
Thee lowly at thy suffering Saviour's feet,
And fill thee with his Holy Spirit's power,
Then use thee as he will.—

      My heart doth ache,
Sometimes to think how we have lost the light
Of thy perpetual presence. Thou wilt dwell
No more amongst us—save at intervals,
And love's bright chain must stretch its links afar;
Yet ne'er, dear brother, by our winter fire
Will we forget thee, and with thoughts of thee,
The calm retiring light of summer eves,
Shall ever mingle at the hour of prayer.

 And now farewell. May covenant blessings rest
Upon thy head in manhood's ripening years;
Earth's honours are but tinsel in thy sight;
I'll wish thee gifts from heaven. If e'er thy name
Fame's trumpet echo in our quiet dales,
Listening, we will not love thee more than now.

1840.

TO A CHILD WEEPING AT ITS
MOTHER'S KNEE.

CHERUB—we watch'd thy blue and laughing eyes
Grave and more grave, with growing ardour fix
On her, thy Mother; and we saw thee press
Near to her side, and nearer, as the tale
Thine infant feelings touch'd, of deep disgrace
And fear that waits on crime, by urchin known
Young as thyself; and then there came sweet words
Of pardon, such as mothers' only grant,
And kiss of love, by love alone denied !
And thou couldst bear no more—the quiet tear
Came trickling, and would come, though brush'd away
In shame, and hidden by the little hand,
Adown thy dimpled cheek.
                                        Ah ! weep, sweet child !
We ne'er so loved thy smile—thy joyous smile.
There hath sprung up within thine heart to-day,
A fount of tender feeling, pity's own,
And memory o'er it seeks to raise a shrine.
On may it flow for ever, till a tide
Of wide philanthropy, noiseless and deep,
'It wind beside all miseries of this world.
Such seems the promise of this early tear
For others' woes.

         Five summers scarce have sunn'd
As yet thy baby brow.   In after years
May none these heart's best feelings e'er repress
By ridicule and scorn.   May she who waked
Their precious source, e'er well-beloved as now,
Fond guide and chosen friend remain, and be
To thee, my brother, all she is to me.

1831.

TO THE SAME,

ON HIS LEAVING ENGLAND FOR AUSTRALIA.

THOU goest—where? departing one,
Thy mother's loved and youngest son;
About to cross the southern deeps,
To a clime that wakes, while Europe sleeps.
In that young continent of hope,
To seek for effort wider scope,
Which now beneath her island skies,
The crowded father-land denies.

Thou goest—where? afar, alone;
Affection, still to boding prone,

Fears that thou oft shalt need the care
Of kindred; wishes thee a share,
'Midst brethren not compell'd to roam
To win the dear delights of home;
Faints at the thought of distance dim,
And weeps to pour thy parting hymn.

The snow is on our summer-seats,
Frozen and chill the vale's retreats;
High piled the logs on winter-fires,
And when their genial blaze expires,
And spring comes forth to walk the woods,
Thy spirit from the pathless floods
Shall send a sigh towards home, while we
Go forth in spirit unto thee.

Yes, we shall miss thy foot-fall light,
Bewail the 'uncle' gay and bright,
Who came at summer eves to tell
Of all that in the town befel.
Recall the mirthful days of yore,
Days of the undivided 'four,'
Whose ringing laughter peals around
The board, our graver voices drown'd.

How one by one, that gamesome crew,
Have parted off in order due!
The parents' home is peaceful left,
The branches all, save one, are cleft;
And but that we, and all our train
Of rising little ones remain,

Their age would lack its fitting stay
At close of life's long labour-day.

Wand'rer, how often wilt thou turn,
When gazing from the vessel's stern,
Towards scenery of our own fair land,
Where late 'twas ours with thee to stand;[1]
With thee and us will still abide
The memories of that mountain-side;
Be Lough Rigg Fell, and Langdale Glen
Our watchwords till we meet again.

Home's spells are on thee, and where'er
Thou goest, we follow thee with prayer;
We know not what temptations may
The vigour of thy faith assay;
May make the wrong the right appear,—
Show thee thyself, and bid thee fear:
The enemy of souls we dread,
But trust in Christ our living head.

God speed thee o'er the ocean's breast,
Provide thee fellowship and rest,
In many a fold across the deep,
Known to the shepherd of the sheep;
And 'midst awaiting whirl of change,
Succession fast of faces strange,
May secret converse with thy Lord,
Daily support and strength afford.

[1] The Westmoreland lakes.

Once we were nine, one hearth beside,
Though now north, south, and west abide
The links of the far-sever'd chain;
Still weal or woe, and joy or pain
Of each, to all is quickly known;
And thou, Belovèd, thou alone,
The blank of silent months must bear,
Though birth or death were passing here.

Still one in thought, and one in hope,
We'll cast thee a bright horoscope;
Go mark the wonders of the deep,
In seas where branching corals sweep.
Let nature all her gifts impart,
Sunrise and sunset touch thine heart;
And, gazing round thee, feast thine eyes
On flowers and stars of southern skies.

If there should chance thy path to cross,
Some sad heart suffering pain or loss;
Be to that heart a friend in need,
Point it to Christ, ' the Friend indeed;'
Make known the Spirit's teaching power,
And peace be with ye in that hour;
Scatter some seed of God's own word,
Where it hath ne'er before been heard.

See much—feel deeply—learn to scan
The dealings of thy fellow man;
Of toil and travel, record keep,
Reward of transient exile reap;

THE YEAR OF RELEASE.

ADDRESSED TO A BELOVED FATHER ON THE DAY OF HIS RETIREMENT
FROM BUSINESS.

FROM Salem's heights in the days of old,
When the blast of silver trumpets roll'd ;
That blast was echoed o'er hill and dale
And all Israel's sons took up the tale,
That the fiftieth year, the jubilee year,
Was come with its balm for sorrow and fear ;
'Twas God's year of release and of liberty,
When the weary might rest, and the slave go free.

'Twas thus, 'twas thus, in the world's young day,
With the chosen race, now cast away ;
It *shall* be thus in Christ's coming reign,
When rebel Judah is born again.
The hard heart of ages, with anguish torn,
Shall ' look upon Him whom she pierced, and mourn;'
And then, her long night of rejection and scorn,
Pass away in the breaking millennial morn !

As yet the Jew hath his birth-right spurn'd,
The Lord hath long to the Gentiles turn'd !
We tread the path that the fathers trod ;
'Tis a progress mark'd and watch'd of God,
And we bend our knee, and we lift our eyes
To the God of the wide world's families,

Who calls us this day in his love and his peace
To honour and welcome the year of release.

Ah! parents dear, and made yet more dear,
As departeth each successive year;
Whose presence soothes in the hour of pain,
Whose sympathy ne'er is sought in vain,
Who knit up the links of affection's chain,
Alway casting them round your numerous train;
We rejoice in your joy whom the morrow cheers,
With farewell to the toil of your fifty years.

A mother's prayers when those years began,
As a sure defence before ye ran;
God heard her prayer for her only son,
And early taught him to raise his own.
Life hath not been to thee a stormy sea,
For the blessing of Heaven hath follow'd thee;
When tempest or peril, or wreck thou hast fear'd,
By thy mother's God, how thy way hath been clear'd!

Leaning throughout on a mighty arm,
So guarded and shelter'd, safe from harm,
From the strife of tongues, and of evil men,
A refuge finding again and again.
What God freely gave thee thou didst not hoard,
But with liberal hand hast scatter'd abroad;
And long as thou livest, thou still wilt believe,
'Tis more blessed to give, than 'tis to receive.

Hail to the hour of calm and repose!
Of quiet and thought, life's evening to close,
With smiles review, yet bedew it with tears,
The map of the mercies of fifty years;
With here a record, and there a stone,
To be read by thee, and thy shepherd alone;
Thy treasure of Time that remaineth shall be
Afresh dedicate, unto Eternity.

And oh! that the blessing which sure is Thine,
May not, dear father, depart from thy line:
May none be missing when God shall claim
The men who have loved and honour'd his name;
Each son, and each daughter, to thee ever given,
Mayst thou humbly lead to thy Father in heaven,
Saying, " Lord, here are all redeem'd by thy love,
All those whom thou gavest me number'd above."

This day—'tis a Pisgah in time's broad waste,
We dare not, we wish not, to pass it in haste,
As on the hill brow, with our parents we stand,
We gaze with desire on the Promised Land:
This steep, in God's strength, they have safely gain'd,
In gentle descent, may they still be sustain'd!
May riches or losses, the smile or the rod,
Bid us each love and trust in our father's God.

1853.

TO OUR ELDER BROTHER,

ON HIS MARRIAGE, MAY, 1837.

A PAGE this morn doth open lie,
New in our household's history;
No record light of infant years,
No tale of childhood's smiles and tears ;
With deeper, tenderer theme it burns,
An eager hand that record turns.

My brother! yes, we haste to meet,
With bridal hymn, and welcome sweet,
The hours which all thine hopes fulfil,
A moment only turn thee still;
One, only one, with us alone,
Back to our father's threshold stone.

Thou art amongst us all, the first
These earliest links of life to burst ;
This threshold thou wilt cross no more,
To feel 'tis home, as heretofore ;
For now another hearth shall be
Fairer and dearer unto thee.

Thy lightsome step we would not stay,
Speed on the wings of joy away!
Go, win thy young and blushing bride!
Without thy Mary at thy side
The lay of love we will not pour,
It wakes for thee alone, no more.

Another heart, another hand
Is added to our circling band,
As one with us, in woe or weal,
And all thine own, this hour doth seal
Her, who will surely sweetly blend,
The names of sister, wife, and friend.

Fond kindred from afar have smiled,
Mary, on thee, their cherish'd child;
Have heard thee softly breathe the vow
Which binds thee to another now;
Thy father's hearth will lonely be
At first, without thy smiles and thee.

See the kind beams in friendship's eye,
As all thy bright young train pass by;
Most whom we love are here; but say,
Does holier presence grace the day?
And seek we Cana's Guest divine,
To turn the water into wine?

One reverend head, whose crown of snow
Is in the quiet grave laid low,
Had oft foretold how holy bands
Would in the future join these hands;

Unseen, perchance he lingers near
And ministers, an angel here.

His way to heaven he meekly trod,
Belovèd, choose your father's God!
Nor from your father's altars turn,
Without a living coal to burn,
When bending at Jehovah's throne,
Ere long ye humbly raise your own.

As yet no cloud around ye lours,
Your earthly path is strewn with flowers;
May every bloom with beauty rife,
Be water'd by the stream of life;
If e'er the thorn amid them rise,
Oh! may it fit ye for the skies.

We shall be scatter'd wide and far,
Perchance as other households are;
But still ' the undivided' pray
For blessings on your heads to-day,
And to the charge of Heaven confide
The parting bridegroom and the bride.

1837.

TO A YOUNG FRIEND,

ON HER MARRIAGE TO A MISSIONARY.

A BRIDE—this is a thrilling word
   To all about to own
The soft and tender ties conferr'd,
   By this one word alone;
The silvery robe, and ring of gold
Should loving heart and hand enfold.

It needs, it needs, a loving heart
   To him, for whom a bride
Consents, with all she loves to part,
   Transplanted to his side;
Her childhood's home for ever leaving,
Her lot with his for ever weaving.

To some the page of life unrolls
   Nor fixes them afar,
The daughter, though a wife, consoles
   Parental hearts, that are
Towards her, as fondly tending still,
As hearts parental ever will.

Yet not to all—such mingling loves,
   A missionary's bride
Forsakes for him her heart approves,
   Sever'd by spaces wide,

'Home, friends, and country,' sister dear,
With thee we thus are parting here.

Didst thou for gold on travel speed
   To India's clime of fire,
Though pearls and rubies were thy meed,
   I could not tune my lyre,
To bid thee pass in gladness on,
It should but wail, that thou wert gone.

'Tis not for gold! A track of light
   Is on the dark blue sea;
Go forth, thy Master doth invite,—
   That track is mark'd for thee;
The balm of Gilead to bestow,
Messenger to the heathen,—go!

Margaret! a nobler lot than thine
   To woman ne'er befals;
'Twere poorly changed, if thou couldst shine
   Empress in palace halls;
Than sent of Jesus to proclaim
In humble love, his saving name.

When He to whom thy plighted vow
   With solemn token seal'd,
For ever surely binds thee now,
   Is weary in the field;
It will be thine to soothe and cheer,
And thine to bid him 'persevere.'

When darkness round him clouds his soul,
   Point to his heavenly light!
Aid him to make the wounded whole,
   And chase the shades of night!
E'er gird him for the fight of faith,
With him be constant unto death!

And He, we trust, will comfort thee,
   Nor chide thee, shouldst thou grieve,
When memories of thy father-land,
   Come over thee, at eve.
Thoughts of its hills, its streams, its trees,
And faces dearer far than these.

'Tis wisely hidden from our sight,
   If e'er we meet again;
Who, amid all this circle bright,
   Would be found missing then.
Time-honour'd heads may rest in clay,
The young may lie as low as they.

Weep not for this, or here or there,
   One Lord we serve and love;
Most blessèd those who win most souls,
   To dwell with him above.
His kingdom come, on life's fair shore,
Nor death nor distance part us more.

1842.

THE BRIDESMAID TO THE BRIDE.

" It was a woe to say Farewell to thee !"

How many a blessing love will breathe,
    Dearest, for thee to-day ;
With many a flower will friendship wreathe,
    And strew thy joyful way.
Friendship and Love shall twine thee chaplet fair,
And thou wilt cherish every tribute there.

Thy joy, beloved of my heart,
    Has long been joy to me ;
Yet when I think this day must part
    For ever—me and thee,
With each glad smile to greet thee as a bride,
Mingles a tear to miss thee from my side.

The day hath dawn'd—a glittering train
    Have trod yon hallow'd aisle :
And when the sun shall rise again,
    Thou and thine own sweet smile
No more shall greet me at thy father's door,
And I shall feel, thou art mine own no more.

Mine own no more—our separate ways
    Henceforth through life we take
Somewhat thou wilt of by-gone days
    Remember for my sake.

To me, my heart's own friend, thy gentle truth
Is link'd with all the happy dreams of youth.

There's not a flower—a wild, wee flower,
　　But music breathes to me;
Memorial of some lonely hour,
　　Pass'd with thy lyre and thee.
No page in Nature's book to me was fair,
Till thou hadst read the beauty written there.

And yet I have not loved thee best
　　For thy lyre's thrilling sound;
More precious still the quiet rest
　　In thy calm spirit found.
Affection's trust and love's serene repose
In free glad converse with the heart it knows.

The few have mark'd thy modest worth,
　　The many knew thee not;
One, dearest now to thee on earth,
　　Seeks that thou share his lot.
Forgive me that mine eyes with tears are dim,
Go pour thine heart's deep treasures out for him.

Go cheer him with thy beaming smile,
　　The halcyon of his nest;
Go charm with every gentle wile
　　The haven of his rest.
Be more to him, if more thou yet canst be,
Be more to him than thou hast been to me.

1832.

BRIDAL CHIMES.

INSCRIBED TO A BROTHER AND SISTER.

I HAD a harp in days of yore,
   With few and simple strings ;
I never dream'd 'twas shadow'd o'er
   With fabled muses' wings.
Apollo lent no classic fire,
It was a wild and homely lyre.

It hung beside my father's door,
   And as affection swept
Its chords Æolian, variously,
   It warbled or it wept.
Meeting with sad or joyous strain,
The mournful or the festal train.

Now to a cot I call my own,
   Transplanted, harp and all,
For hours of leisure long and lone,
   The muse in vain might call,
If ere she stepp'd this rural way,
And deign'd upon *my* harp to play.

Yet is my heart no colder grown
   To those I loved of old ;

It mingles in their joys and woes,
  With sympathies untold.
And now and then the harp will break
Its wonted silence—for their sake.

This bridal day divides and binds
  With solemn vow and seal,—
Two loved ones from the kindred bands,
  Who have been wont to kneel
One altar round—it must divide
To bind them to each other's side.

Now welcome to connubial state,
  Brother and sister dear;
Ye enter it with hope elate,
  Chastised by holy fear.
When bridal glitter wanes away,
Deeper and tenderer feelings stay.

'Tis not a path so thornless found,
  As hope unchasten'd dreams;
Yet oh! how fair its measured bound,
  To hearts united seems!
For sin subdued, and self denied,
Can make its bliss, whate'er betide.

Go, pluck each flower that strews your way,
  God bids them blossom there,
Fair seeds, and few, from Eden's bowers,
  Left in this world of care.

If thorns shall wound, his love can heal,
That love both brier and flower reveal.

For you, may every fleeting year
   But faster knit these ties;
Suffering can each to each endear,
   And train ye for the skies.
And joys, those joys *together* known,
Will double all ye felt alone.

High aims are yours, and firm intent,
   One Lord ye love and serve;
You and your household will be bent,
   His statutes to observe.
Order and peace, a dove-like pair,
Shall fold their wings and nestle there.

Moving amid the world's vain crowd,
   Ye will be separate found,
Pilgrims confest, set forth for heaven,
   And there in earnest bound:
Oft winning wanderers by the way,
But making for yourselves no stay.

Earth's fairest cup is dash'd with gall,
   Clouds streak its brightest sky;
Else might it prove the Christian's *all*,
   And ne'er his soul should fly,
To taste the cup of heavenly bliss,
And seek for brighter skies than this.

Yet fair your cup, and bright your sky,
    Beloved, blessings be,
On all God's bounteous hand hath shower'd,
    Abundant, choice, and free—
Till ye shall reach Heaven's sacred shore,
And, ' full of blessing,' need no more.

1841.

THE NEW HOME.

ADDRESSED TO * * * * AND * * * * * ON THEIR WEDDING DAY.

PLEASANT and bright the flower-strewn way,
    By which the bridegroom leads the bride
To her new home, in fair array,
    Shrining her there in love and pride.
The thought shall prompt a bridal lay,
To those such home awaits to-day.

We walk'd of late amidst its bowers,
    Soft silent welcomes there we found,
The music of the sunset hours,
    Was breathing from the landscape round.
Where lake-like river far away,
Received the sinking orb of day.

Blue distant hills and rich champaign
 The site commands, and, wondrous birth,
The railroad sweeping o'er the plain,
 Man's giant march o'er God's wide earth;
Beyond, the Thames, on its broad breast
Cradles the wealth of East and West.

And, oh! how fair in nearer view
 The village spire, the dark wood side,
The smoke of hamlet curling blue,
 The old grey tower that elm-trees hide;
Such tranquil scenes have softening power,
Uncounted gold is poorer dower.

The sunrise and the eventide
 In that sweet home of peace and rest,
Await the bridegroom and the bride,
 When they shall reach their shelter'd nest;
The silvery moon look'd in awhile,
For those on whom she soon should smile.

And here, we thought, there shall unfold
 Life's mingled page of joys and cares,
For these young hearts of loving mould,
 Dear children of their father's prayers;
Here a new altar rise to heaven,
For all the gifts their God has given.

Here may they learn to know the Lord,
 And feel his Spirit's influence high,
13

May rule their household by his word,
   And walk with him, confidingly;
Chastised in mercy by the rod,
If they forsake their father's God.

And if most dear the earthly joy
   Each in the other's heart shall find,
'Twill nothing of that bliss destroy,
   To taste it with a heavenly mind:
The happiest home is but a tent,
To pilgrims on their journey lent.

We welcome Thee with earnest heart,
   Sweet sister, thy new home to grace,
Thy smiles far more than aught beside,
   Will shed a brightness round the place;
In summer walks, by winter fires,
We picture thee, with glad desires.

Thou com'st to fill in part the void,
   Made by our scattering wide and far;
Ten years ago, we number'd nine,
   Divided now, as others are—
But one or two will soon remain,
In their old home, of all the train.

From time to time in mingling glee,
   Our father's hearth in turn receives
Each branch once sever'd from the tree,
   With added graft, and shoots, and leaves;

Nor yet hath any bitter root
Unto that hearth borne bitter fruit.

So ever parting and renewing,
  Are the frail links of earth and time;
May every change to each ensuing
  Prepare them for that purer clime,
Where, mortal needs and sorrows o'er,
E'en marriages are made no more.

1848.

APRIL FOOLS.

SUGGESTED BY THE DEEP SNOW AND FROST OF THE FIRST OF

APRIL, 1830.

WHEN Spring was abroad, one last of March,
She met with two urchins looking arch,
   Saunt'ring together to school;
And she heard of the glorious trick they had plann'd
Against Master, who's always so grave and so grand,
   To make him an April Fool.

It enter'd into her frolicsome head,
By the same small imp of mischief sped,
   Who all merry children rules,
That, just to divert her for four or five hours,
She would mask like winter, and frighten the flowers,
   And make *them* April Fools.

'Twas a costly prank; for each dark stem
She had pointed, with an emerald gem,
   Swelling in tender pride:
Had call'd to every bud to discard
Fold after fold of its russet shard;
   And could these a frost abide?

The hyacinth bells, to the humming bees,
Had been chiming long in the open breeze;
  ' They'll shiver,' she said, ' with fear :
The jonquil stars have made bold to blow,
So I'll fill their small gold cups with snow,
  Or an icicle cool and clear.'

The morning came ; and when men arose
They gazed on December's pathless snows,
  And spoke of a changeful clime ;
And the furs they had doff'd with the winter's reign
All closely they folded about them again,
  And pitied the garden's prime.

One cannot say that one grieved sincerely,
Inasmuch as one never loved them dearly,
  For the flaring daffodillies ;
But *they* look'd half modest, while drooping their heads
So resignedly down on the sparkling beds,
  Low as the vale's sweet lilies.

The young leaves whisper'd their wild amaze,
And ask'd each other what sunbright days
  Had tempted them out at all ;
And the sleet fell fast on the blackbird's wing,
Tho' we heard him, trying to think it was spring,
  To his mates in melody call.

Pale fear into every primrose crept,
Whole purple violet households wept,

And shrank in wild affright :
While nectarine and peach in the utter gloom,
Were show'ring in haste their untimely bloom,
   All through the bitter night.

Flies had been flitting, and musical trill
The robin had utter'd by wood and rill :
   We had hail'd the yellow moth,
On the rough wind's pinions his death-sigh sped,
For his delicate winglets soil'd and dead—
     Fairies, O Spring! were wroth!

The merry Spring had such mischief made,
That she truly rued the prank she had play'd ;
   And for two whole days and a night
She tried to weep it away in rain :
But if Flora should never believe her again,
   Now would it not serve her right?

THE SPRING TO THE WINTER

OF 1837.

My kingdom, my kingdom!—stern Winter, I say,
I'm coming to claim it, and turn thee away;
I've waited and waited, the time to afford
Thee, to part and begone of thine own accord;
But thou lovest, I see, to be master and lord!
      And ne'er thou wilt go,
      With thy frost and snow,
      If thou hast thine own will,
      And I bear with it still.
   November, December, are thine,
   But April and May they are mine!

Away, then away, to thine icebergs away!
And let me and my breezes come freely play!
We must fan every leaflet and blossom delay'd
In its prisoning sheath, of thy frowns afraid.
Ah! thy sear blue fingers have over them stray'd.
      Buds never were thine!
      Save those of the pine;
      Nor thy sky, grey and dark,
      For my soaring lark!

My treasures—do thou let alone
I pray thee, and keep to thine own.

Thy mantle is ermine, with icicles fringed;
Leave me the green velvet with buttercups tinged;
Thy zone is of diamonds, and mine is of flowers.
Ah, me! thou hast linger'd so long in my bowers,
I shall ne'er, e'en now, with my sunbeams and showers,
  Have garlands to greet
  The young dancing feet,
  Which will merrily bound
  My bright throne around!
 Thou'rt surely not plotting to stay
And frighten my children away!

My bees! they are starving! yes, monster, behold
In their beautiful cells, they lie dead with cold.
The few who crawl forth are too weary and weak
From cup, bud, or bell, at my bidding to seek
The nectar that feeds them—Oh! hence in a week
  I'll scare thee, old churl!
  Thou must fold and furl!
  Hence thy vaporous shroud!
  And make way for a crowd
 Of gay forms, at once to have birth,
On the waking and jubilant earth.

Here I am, with the lark in his carollings wild;
Here I am, with my celandine, hardiest child!
That for ever comes dropping its sparklets of gold
Where the daisy yet dares not, o'er wood and o'er wold;

Before my fair sunlight thy shadows have roll'd.
    And now for warm showers
    To cherish my flowers,
    Till all glowing, they burst,
    As in Eden at first;
  I'll breathe o'er the world in a day,
And send tidings to every spray.

One word, as thou fliest, I whisper thee still:
Thou shalt not return at thy mischievous will,
To peril one bud that in me doth confide!
If thou should'st for an hour, to thee is denied,
In ages to come, what to me is allied.
    Nor e'er thy dark train
    Will I broider again,
    Or hem it with light
    By my snowdrops bright.
  Usurper! thou rulest no more!
  My kingdom, my kingdom—restore!

April 20.

PRIMROSES.

"Primroses, the Spring may love them."—*Wordsworth*.

'LOVE them?' yes; and well she may,
Such as we have seen to-day!
  First with glee espied,
Scarcely golden, scarcely white,
Thickly sprinkled, starry bright,
  Upon the far hill-side.

Faster urged along the lanes,
Pony Dapple felt the reins,
  Oft he wonder'd why.
Violet banks on former days,
Celandines had claim'd our praise,
  Now we pass'd them by.

Till that coppice steep attain'd,
He, free will to nibble gain'd,
  Left to wander on;
Strolling up its alleys wild,
Each with heart of joyous child,
  Our gamesome crew were gone.

Such a sight ne'er seen before,
Plucking till we could no more,
  We had primrose fill;
Fair, large blossoms, each the other
Fairer, larger than its brother,
  Lured us farther still.

Guessing not our rude employ,
Gazing up at us with joy,
  Every primrose bland;
Till recalling poet's faith,
That ' e'en a flower enjoys its breath,'
  I staid my cruel hand.

Change unto the eye was none,
All the thousands blooming on,
  Ne'er their neighbours missing:
Scarce a sunbeam mark'd the wrong,
Down the hazel-wands among,
  Where he each was kissing.

Mary! avaricious grown,
Let that queenly root alone!
  Hist! I heard it say,
' Here a lone, wood-life, it lingers,
Better die by fairy fingers:'
  Bear it then away!

Wood anemones are bright,
We have seen them fair and slight,

Droop in flocks around
Where the axe the oak has laid,
And green moss its couch has made,
  They are blushing found.

Violets! both white and blue,
Hearts will ever dance for you,
  In the hedge-rows wild;
Listen not with envious ear,
If, on this day of all the year,
  Primroses have smiled.

1837.

TO A YOUNG FRIEND

ON HIS BIRTH-DAY, IN THE MERRY MONTH OF MAY.

My very dear Jasper,
The birds in May
Have talk'd with each other
Of you to-day;
I listen'd and heard,
Though I am not a bird,
What they said to the flowers
Which April showers
Had scatter'd in flocks
Over meadows and rocks;
While the country round
Was o'erflowing with sound.

The hawk he wink'd
With his eagle eye,
And he said to a nettle
Which grew hard by,
' We'll take this wight,
And we'll teach him aright,
To carp and to scan,
And to find in man
All the fault he can.
For the youth is sharp,
And his looks are arch,
And by rights he should
Have been born in March.

From this day forth
His wit shall be
Sparkling and piercing
In keen degree;
Further than most
This boy shall see;
He shall wear a sting,
And prove early wise,
And the world shall be
Foolish in his eyes.'

I do not know
What else to bestow
This pair intended,
For ere they had ended,
All the birds beside
Against them cried!
The robin dared,
And the goldfinch shared
In his hardy trill
To dispute the will
Of the hawk with the eagle eye;
The merry brown linnet
Saw mischief in it;
The thrush could not rest
In her woodland nest,

Nor the cuckoo forego,
Her claim to bestow,
On the day of your birth
The stamp of mirth;
And each wee thing,
That was born in the spring,
Said you were theirs,
That they saw in your eye,
Something that shares
In gladness and joy;
And they bade it beam kindly
And oftentimes blindly,
Where the hawk
Would have had it rest,
And sent you on happier quest,
In search of whatever was best
Of goodness and worth,
Sprinkled over the earth.

They thought that the hawk
With the eagle eye,
Might teach you a lesson
Perhaps by and by.
But as yet you should sing
With the birds in the spring,
Of the lightness and brightness
Which Maytime doth bring.

Now, forgive me this jingle;
Its aim has been single,
Dear Jasper, to prove
True friendship and love;
For in age and in youth,
I desire to remain
In affection and truth
Yours ever, L. N.

THE FIND-FAULT BOX;

OR,

THE HABIT OF CENSURE.

" It is very easy to find fault." I remember a reproof being once conveyed to me in these words, when I was remarking the imperfections in a school-fellow's drawing: " I love," continued our kind governess, " that amiable feeling, especially in young people, which, when it cannot commend, is silent. We need never violate sincerity, or oppose our judgment by praising that which is undeserving of praise; but, my dear child, as you pass through life, seek for beauties rather than for faults in the works of others; for a critical temper is unpleasing in the sight of God, and will never ensure you the good-will of your fellow-creatures."

In after life, I had not unfrequent opportunities of communication with a family whom, if I introduce at first to my young readers, in an unamiable light, it is with an earnest prayer that they may turn away from this picture, and its painful colours, to exhibit in their own deportment, in stronger contrast, the "gentleness which is in Jesus Christ."

"Mother! I wish you would give that lazy housemaid warning; making me ring three times, when I know she saw me long before I came to the gate at all." These words, in an angry tone, announced the appearance of a young gentleman at the dinner hour to his mother and sisters who were waiting for him.

"My dear James," said his mother, with a smile, "that is a mistake; Susan is scrubbing at the back of the house; I heard you ring but once, and then begged your sister Emily to let you in."

"She is a tiresome, whining, uncomfortable, good-for-nothing creature; I'd not keep such a maid, I know."

"Well, James," said Emily, "now you are let in, do not trouble yourself to give the maids warning; but come to your dinner, and tell us what is happening out of doors."

"You should read the newspaper for yourself, sister, and not teaze me."

"We have been mending your shirts, brother, and reading Caroline Fry, on Good Humour, which I think I shall serve up, for your sake, at dessert."

"Yes! you mend my things, and buy new ones for yourself. Did I not tell you yesterday, I chose to wear studs instead of buttons? and here are the buttons still. You can look out for the fashions yourself, but I may be dressed like my grandfather."

"Brother, brother," said Emily, "that is not true; it is my turn to be cross now."

"No, Emily," said her mother, "two are not better than one, in this case. I will praise you, as much as you please, and make up for James's deficiencies; but oh! my children, what will become of you, unless this habit of censure, which you imbibe the one from the other, is checked and overcome? When will it please God to soften your hearts, and cause this evil spirit to come out of you?"

For many months had this affectionate mother sighed in secret over the evil which she now deplored. It was as she said, the habit of her children never to pass by anything which they observed, or imagined to be wrong in each other; and, although they were not all really ill-natured, even the youngest was perpetually making some tart remark, which was sure to occasion irritation, and retort from the individual attacked.

It is not possible for very quiet and kind-hearted people, who take things easily, to conceive of the atmosphere which these frequent collisions of feeling created. It was certainly the very opposite to the gentleness of Christian love; but at the time of which I speak, this family could not be called a Christian family; that "faith, which worketh by love," was not possessed by any of its junior members; their mother had been left a widow during their childhood; and with the natural meekness which might have endeared her to her children, she unhappily did not combine the judicious firmness which must check in the bud those manifestations of inward corruption that often arise even in well-ordered families.

14

An old friend, who knew something of their internal disagreements, and loved them well enough to desire their improvement, one day brought them an ebony box, divided into two compartments, with an aperture in each, for the admission of a penny.

It was not exactly a collecting-box, or it collected on a singular principle, the principle of conscience and self-condemnation. In ivory letters, upon the lid, was this inscription :—

"FOR BITTER AND IDLE WORDS."

Over one aperture was written—

"OF THE ABSENT."

Over the other—

"TO THE PRESENT."

The friend who brought this box was an old gentleman, of very mild and polished manners, whom they highly esteemed, and whose company they valued and desired. He had felt so grieved by their habit of finding fault, that, much as he was pleased with the talent, the wit, and general intelligence he found by their fireside, he felt that he must forsake it unless this evil could be ameliorated : he thought he should prefer this method of reproof to any form of advice or remonstrance, for he had observed that it is more important to lead young people to correct themselves than to set about correcting them.

He had noticed, according to his own favourite custom, various good points in their character; and he thought that some of them were open to conviction, and would soon see the benefit of a self-imposed restriction upon their liberty of speech. With the gift, he requested that two or three rules might be established : First, that no person, except the head of the family, should decide for another on the duty of a forfeit to the box. Secondly, that it should always be in sight, and accessible to visitors. Thirdly, that reproach upon contribution should never be allowed, on penalty of a double fine.

" I think," said James to their friend, " this will greatly check the freedom of conversation; for even supposing that the failings of those present must pass unobserved, (which, I think, would make us all very tame and conceited,) one must often speak of the absent, and how is it possible always to speak well?"

" Try it," said the old gentleman; " the forfeit is not for all manner of speech, but only for 'idle and bitter words.'"

On the day when the box was to commence its silent monitorship, the family met at breakfast, and were speaking of a party of friends, at which some of them had been present on the previous evening, who were accustomed to assemble monthly for the discussion of moral and religious subjects. Their topic on this occasion had been—" The union of activity and repose in Christian character." As the box was in sight, remarks and remembrances were of a favourable nature, until Emily, forgetting its presence, said,

" I do not wonder that Mrs. Wynn should have taken the side of ' repose.' She is so still and inactive. She does nothing herself, and is always afraid that others should do too much."

The words were spoken,—they could not be recalled, and they were the property of the box; for if not bitter, they were idle and unnecessary : and when Emily afterwards knew more of Mrs. Wynn, and found that her calm and devotional spirit was perpetually, yet quietly, enlisted in the service of her meek and lowly Master, she remembered and grieved over the cause of this her first contribution.

" I do not know," said James, " whether this speech of

Mrs.Wynn be true or not true; but I do know some people whose character is so bad that it would be kindness to them to take it away, and let them get another,—such men now as Mr. Harding. What a hypocrite he is! and what a cheat! and how ill he treats his wife!"

A universal testimony to the ill deserts of Mr. Harding was being given, when mamma said to her little Jane, a lively girl of nine years old, " My child, you are eating too much butter; and where is your pinafore this morning?"

" Oh, mamma," was the answer, " go to the Find-fault Box."

Of course this was set down to the score of playfulness or of ignorance; but, as the old gentleman that day dined with them, the mother referred to him if he meant to include, under the head of finding fault, any observations she might see ·fit to make on what was wrong in her children. He immediately decided in the negative, and even wondered at the reference; " because," he added, " the reproofs of a parent like yourself, my dear madam, can never be 'bitter or idle words,' but always tokens of your love and interest in the individual you address; this must likewise apply to all who have the direction and guidance of youth. My aim is, to check them in finding fault with each other."

" And pray, Sir," said James, " may not one speak ill of people who deserve it? Mr. Harding, for instance."

" I do not decide for you, my young friend; I feel that I never may speak ill even of those who deserve it, unless I am called upon to warn others against them. If I am convinced that a man is a dishonest lawyer, it is my duty to prevent a friend from taking his advice; but I should never think it a privilege to do so. 'Charity rejoiceth not in iniquity.'"

" How are we, then," said Emily, " to have anything like

discrimination of character, if we may never mention its distinctive points ? "

"If you come to the subject intellectually and morally, I
do not say, avoid distinctive points; if you are speaking of
an excellence or a failing in the abstract, you must often
instance it, in an individual in whom it strikingly exists; but
whenever this can be done by referring to actions without
names, I think it is best. 'It is more safe to speak of things
than of persons.'"

"I have one more question to ask," said James, "and
then I will put in my fine for Mr. Harding. Are people of
quick and keen observation—I mean in little things—obliged
to pass by without notice, a hundred little awkward habits in
those with whom they associate, just as if these habits did
not exist at all ? "

"My dear James," said the old gentleman, "do not make
me lawgiver for you. You must judge for yourself, whether
the unsparing notice of these little annoyances, by a young
person among his equals, does not induce in himself a habit
worse than any which he condemns, the habit of censure.
Few people are the better for being continually 'rasped
down'; and it will be more easy to obviate what we do not
like in others, by an opposite example, than by any war of
words. I have remarked, that those who are most 'apt to
teach' the young, the humble, and the ignorant, do not
perpetually find fault with them. And with regard to awk-
wardness, does it ever make a person less awkward to laugh
at him ? "

Here the conversation dropped; but the holy and gentle
influence of this kind friend, silently proceeded in sowing the
good seed, which afterwards sprang up, and brought forth
fruit abundantly.

His was one of those

> " Strong minds
> Of whom the noisy world hears least,
> Beloved and honoured, far as he was known.
> And some small portion of his eloquent speech,
> His observations, and the thoughts his mind
> Had dealt with,"—

they love to record, now that his head is laid low in the sepulchre of his fathers.

James and Emily gradually softened down, and became as amiable as they were intelligent; the trial of the box convinced them daily that "the tongue can no man tame," and was one means of leading them to the fountain of forgiveness for all sin; it led them to watch and to pray at the foot of the cross. The sorrows of life have touched them—for whom do these sorrows spare?—but these have only drawn them closer together, and brought them nearer to God. May this little sketch of their early days be of some benefit to those who desire to walk in the "strait and the narrow way, which leadeth unto life everlasting."

1838.

A PONY'S OBITUARY.

RHYMES ADDRESSED TO BROTHERS AT SCHOOL.

DEAR Robert and Sam,
How sorry I am,
To have to impart,
What must grieve the heart
Of every boy,
Who had e'er the joy,
To ride or to drive,
A pony alive,
At his own wild will,
Over dale and hill,
With a laugh and a gibe
At the rocking-horse tribe.

Ah, brethren bold!
To have and to hold
Such a pony alive,
To ride and to drive
Was once your lot;
But was and is not.
Poor Sandy's no more!
Leave your learnèd lore,
Your own grey Sandy,
Your dear little Sandy,
Sandy's no more!

Leave Latin and Greek
With a tear on your cheek,
And dry mathematics,
To students in attics;
And while your eyes glisten,
Alas! come and listen
While I shall you tell
The fate that befel,
Your poor little Sandy,
Your dear grey Sandy,
Sandy's no more!

The chalk-pit, I ween
You guess where I mean;
The chalk-pit you know,
You have look'd down below
At its sides so steep,
And fearfully deep,
From the green hill-top,
At the risk of a pop
Over the edge
Of the dizzy ledge;
Well—holiday fun,
Being over and done,

And you at your books,
With industrious looks :
It was thought to make Sandy
Both useful and handy,
And put him to work
In carting some chalk,
From its snowy white bed,
In the pit aforesaid,
And teach him to travel
Towards pit of gravel,
Along the hill-top
Without making a stop.

Charles Emery drove him,
And tried to improve him;
For they said he was idle,
Nor minded the bridle;
And would often stand still,
On the top of the hill,
(I've no doubt it was true,)
And be thinking of you.

Thus it was, but last week,
Or strictly to speak,
Last Friday, this way
He chose to delay
His business for play.
Charles Emery " whack'd"
And Sandy he back'd ;
Not knowing his danger,
Unfortunate stranger
To perils of pits,
And half out of his wits

He back'd, cart and all,
There was death in the fall.
Charles Emery " tried
As he near'd the steep
   side,
To catch or to snatch,
At the horse or the cart,
It was well for his part,
He was not over too."
If his story be true,
Ere a word could be spoken,
Poor Sandy's neck broken,
Cart " shatters "—as well,
Lay down in the dell.
In mercy they shot
The poor beast on the spot.
Oh ! think of his moans,
And his misery's groans,
And now weep o'er his bones.

Mamma was at dinner,
Charles Emery—a sinner,
Did not like to tell Master
About the disaster,
Until they had finish'd ;
Lest hunger diminish'd
Should flee at his tale,
Then he came with a wail,
And they sought the dark
   dell
Where poor Sandy fell,
And mourn'd as of old
Did Fitz-James the bold,

When his gallant grey,
By Loch Katrine lay.

I have no more time,
To tell you in rhyme
The things that have past, .
Since we wrote to you last;

But must leave it to others,
Or sisters or brothers;
I entreat you believe,
That with love I remain,
Poor Sandy's biographer,
Sister L. N.

1836.

A CORONER'S INQUEST.

" FOUND DROWNED."

In a vase which graced a garden's bound,
There were three butterflies " found drown'd."
A fetter'd eagle of yore was known
To lave his wings in that font of stone;
But his chain was riven, his font was dry,
And its use scarce holden in memory,
Except when a shower of passing rain
Might fill it, for lesser birds again;
Such lake of summer the insects spied,
And, ah! in its mimic depths they died.

It chanced these butterflies had been
The frolic steeds of the fairy queen,
Who whiles she will'd at drowsy noon
To dream in the cactus cups of pine,

Had slipp'd her gossamer rein to rove,
Like flying flowers around the grove.
" Primroses," poets said of Spring,
" In their living forms had taken wing."

Titania, when her dream was done,
Her coursers sought, at set of sun;
And she wept such tears as fairies weep,
When she found them sleeping solemn sleep
Within that font, so cold and deep.

Ken ye how fair is the moonlight beam?
Which loves 'mid night's dun shades to stream?
Softly it fell with a silvery light
On the folded wings of the dead that night;
When the naiad who made the font her care,
Woke to the tread of the spirits of air,
And listed the musical tones and low,
Which fays through trumpets of woodbine blow.
'Twas Oberon's queen, on the lake's calm shore,
Alighted to mourn her steeds no more,
And twelve fair brothers were in her train,
Of the lifeless, stretch'd on the glassy plain.

They waked each bird from its midnight rest,
To summon its aid in their anxious quest,
The cause of this fell mischance of death!
Did any receive the parting breath?
Had a naughty gnome on the marge that play'd
For mischief, their merry wanderings laid?

Or was it that the conceited elves
Had caught the reflection of themselves
In the still waters' treacherous face,
Deceived, as are others of their race,
Who, frantic worshippers of fire,
For love of light, in flames expire?

Could a boding dream, in evil hour
Have come o'er them, with malignant power!
Sear leaves of Autumn did they dread
To be whirl'd upon their dying head,
In an eventide of lurid red?
So thought to scape such stormy time,
By dying with Summer, in her prime?
" Foresight like this," the fairy said,
" Was an organ not in a butterfly's head."

Perchance they deem'd, from existence past,
That life in all *varied forms* could last:
Remembering how their wings of gold,
Once in a filmy shroud could fold.
They thought from another grave to rise,
On the bird's strong pinion through the skies;
Yet, nay! for ambition's steep to climb
Was never yet an insect's crime.

One gloomy guess remain'd beside;
Was it of broken hearts they died?
The jurors twelve, the car forsaking
Of their bright queen, were then betaking

Themselves to each enchanting Fair,
To ask if she the tyrant were
That urged the wretched to despair?

There came a hush'd, disdainful sound,
From all the waken'd flowers around;
The lily toss'd her lovely head,
The white rose blush'd in anger red;
The balsam, with her hundred dyes,
The jasmine, with her starry eyes;
Convolvulus that shuns the moon,
Wakes with the dawn, and fades at noon:
All beauties that in turn had smiled
A moment on such suitors wild,
Haughty and careless did declare,
'Twas never worth their while to snare
These fickle children of the air.
A zephyr's privilege they craved,
Scorn'd as he scorn'd, to be enslaved;
Gloried, that neither bud nor bell
Held elfin charm, or mutter'd spell,
Their stray devotions to compel.
The flowers replied, Go wander free,
Our heart's deep love is not for ye,
We keep it for the constant bee.

Titania sought no more to prove
That her butterflies had died for love.

What final verdict they had found,
I know not; it was lost in sound,

Betiding the approach of morn.
A gnat's reveille of humming horn,
He was the Fairy's bugler born.
The flitting of the shadows gray,
The coming of the streaks of day;
They waited only till they heard,
The first soft chirping of the bird;
Key-note of that inspiring strain,
Which night alone will hush again.
Off in a fright the fairy flew,
The jury all adjourn'd.—Adieu!

1833.

A SONG FOR SCHOOL-CHILDREN.

Air—" Twinkle, twinkle, little star."

SPRINKLE, sprinkle, little shower,
Pearly drops on every flower!
Each fair daisy opes its eye,
Gladly as thou passest by.

See! the grass that should be green,
Where the burning sun has been,
How it looks all brown and bare!
Sprinkle, sprinkle, kindly there.

Hark, the earth is calling loud,
For the treasures of the cloud!
Loves the sun, but wants the rain;
Pleasant shower, oh, come again!

Sprinkle, sprinkle, where the corn,
In its young green shoot is born!
Sprinkle, sprinkle, where the grass,
Is not so tall but we may pass.

When we toss the new-mown hay,
Pleasant shower, oh, keep away;
Do not wet the sheaves of gold
When the harvest months are told!

Just the dusty pathway cool,
Leading to our happy school;
When the hour for play is o'er,
Sprinkle, sprinkle then no more.

God, who never doeth ill,
Sends thee at his gracious will;
Thank him, thank him for the rain,
Thank him for the sun again.

A BABY'S LETTERS TO HIS FRIENDS.

No. 1.

TO AUNT ISABEL ON HER BIRTHDAY.

AUNT ISABEL, Aunt Isabel,
    My youngest aunt, my best;
I call you best, yet do not mean
    Offence to all the rest;
I call you best, because you seem
    Not quite so tall and high,
And so you are more fit to nurse
    So small a thing as I.

Aunt Isabel! I heard them say,
    (You see I use my ears,)
That you are twelve years old to-day;
    What do they mean by " years ? "
I number days and weeks, you know,
    I'm a month old, and more;
Whene'er the daylight comes, I crow
    That the dark night is o'er.

I heard Mamma, or Mrs. Burn,
    (But which I cannot tell,)
Wishing this day might oft return
    To you Aunt Isabel!

And, do you know, this very day,
  Mamma has drest me first;
I always scream, but I have tried
  To scream not quite my worst.

Oh! I hate water!—Did not you,
  When you were young as I?
And all that they think right to do,
  Which I must bear, and be,
As quiet as I can, dear Aunt!
  You know that I *must* cry
To tell them what I like and want;
  I cannot speak, not I.

I came into this world, I think,
  To eat, and sleep, and grow;
Perhaps I've something more to do,—
  You'll tell me, if you know.
And now farewell, Aunt Isabel,
  Believe, where'er you are,
Your little nephew loves you well,
  His name is Ernest R.

February, 1840.

No. 2.

TO COUSIN PHILIP.

Dear Cousin Philip! How do you do?
I liked the day I spent with you,
   A little nursery guest;
But now my London visit's o'er,
They say I shall not see you more
   For a long while at least.

They call you " Baby,"—that's the name
That people give—the very same—
   To me as well as you;
Yet you are larger far than I,
And wiser too, undoubtedly,
   I wonder why they do?

It seems that you can almost walk,
And then I heard you almost talk;
   Oh! Oh! you said to me.
You gave a look of glad surprise,
And then you tried to poke my eyes
   To find if I could see.

This morning I've to Hampstead been
And your dear grandmamma have seen,
   And thank'd her for my cloak;
My fine long trains are fair to see,

15

But oh! they sadly trouble me,
  And fashion seems a joke.

Well, ere I leave Great Ormond-street,
(I'm going to the daisies sweet,
  In my green native vale,)
I thought I'd send to say adieu,
Dear Philip, to Mamma and you,
  With pen from goldfinch' tail.

If you should like this pony white,
He's free to serve you day and night,
  And " Trusty" is his name ;
He's sure of foot ; your nursery floor
I hope he oft will bear you o'er,
  But do not run him lame.

Good-by, dear Philip ; summer 's nigh,
And then I hope that you and I
  Shall on green grass-plot meet,
Where you shall run, and I shall roll,
And ere six months have o'er me stole
  I mean to feel my feet.

Good-by once more ; and when astride
On Trusty's back you learn to ride,
  Be sure you think sometimes
Of cousin Ernest, far away,
Who says whate'er he has to say
  In jingles and in rhymes.

March, 1840.

No. 3.

TO AUNT ELIZABETH.

Dear Aunt Elizabeth, I thought
  This morning as I lay
Within the pretty curtain'd bed
  I owe to you, they say—
I thought so many thoughts, I'll try
  To tell you, one by one,
Tho' most folks would have past me by,
  And guess'd that I had none.

I thought—It is the first green spot
  Which I can call my own;
Soft is my sleep, and sweet my dreams,
  As there I lie alone.
And then at waking oft I hear
  The birds sing merrily,
Or list that music [1] low and clear,
  Which seems just made for me.

They place me in my bassinette,
  Wherein I sink to rest:
The cool air fans against my face,
  And I'm no sooner drest,

---

[1] A musical box.

And out in our fair garden ground,
   Than, much against my will,
Closing my eyes on all around
   I'm sleepy, sleepy, still.

This morning I am three months old!
   And oh! I feel so strong—
I wish they'd sing, and let me dance,
   I'm sure, the whole day long.
They've borne me in the sunny beams,
   I heard glad voices round,
And smelt the sweet and pleasant flowers,
   Mamma had for me found.

' Heartsease and violets,' do you know
   Such strange hard names as these?
And ' daffodils' in golden row,
   My eye already please.
Bird of the bowers, I love the flowers,
   The heavens are bright and blue,
I'm come into a pleasant world
   I think, dear Aunt, don't you?

Papa is very kind to me,
   I've learn'd at him to smile
As in his arms I silent lie,
   He whistling all the while.
My little goldfinch quill he gave
   I keep it in my cot,
To write a letter now and then,
   In that dear quiet spot.

There's sameness in my style, I fear,—
  O dear, I've just found out
A "heartsease on my curtains here,
  And it smells sweet, no doubt;
Thank you, dear Aunt, for making me
  So nice a bed as this is;
To save the post in haste this comes,
  With Ernest's thanks and kisses.

April 1840.

No. 4.

ERNEST TO GRANDPAPA R.,

ON HIS SEVENTIETH BIRTHDAY.

Aunt Sara tells me, Grandpapa,
  That this eighteenth of June,
When pinks and roses blooming round
  Make Midsummer's bright noon,
She tells me seventy years ago
  This day, that you were born,
A Baby—very much like me,
  All helpless and forlorn.

'Tis very strange, 'tis wondrous strange,
  To think that such things are!
Suppose now I should ever grow
  Into a Grandpapa!

I must believe Aunt Sara, yet
  I scarcely can suppose
That you, so old a man, were e'er
  A baby in long clothes.

My droll Papa has made a speech
  All about beer and wine,
For me to speak to grandchildren,
  In years to come of mine.
He says, " Such drinks will not be known
  When seventy years are fled;
When nought but water rules the land,
  And alcohol is dead."

I love to sit and listen long,
  When wondrous tales are told.
And when to Richmond I shall come,
  If I may make so bold,
I'll sit upon your knee, and hear,
  If you will tell to me,
Some stories of your seventy years,
  And be so still, you'll see.

I speak as people round me speak;
  They say that " change and care,"
Must come with threescore years and ten,
  And sorrow, hard to bear.
But " change," and " care," and " woe," are words
  That nothing mean to me;
I lead a life so like a bird's,
  Hopping from tree to tree.

Aunt Sara says, dear Grandpapa,
   You have been ill; I'll try
To trouble you, if I should come,
   But little by my cry.
I scarce can tell what ' illness' means,
   Except 'tis ' vaccination,'
And sure they have not scratch'd your arm,
   That cruel operation.

Adieu! I hope you'll soon be well,
   Or better, this fine weather,
And then we shall enjoy July,
   The close of it together.
I yesterday was five months old;
   My love to grandmamma,
If she perchance enquire for me,
   Your loving Ernest R.

No. 5.

TO A FRIEND, WITH AN ALBUM.

Dear Sidney More! my future friend,
   Pray take this little book,
And think of Ernest now and then,
   When you shall in it look.
Ernest, who wishes you to be
   (He speaks as he is told)
What your mamma to his mamma
   Was in the days of old.

My " future friend,"—I do not know
  Exactly what this means;—
Perhaps it will be clearer made,
  As we approach our " teens:"
And meeting at some famous school,
  Shall each so love the other,
That you to me shall dearer be
  Than brother is to brother.

My friends at present, I believe,
  Are " Peter," " Burr," and " Jack."
Peter's a donkey, with long ears,
  And baskets on his back;
He travels round our garden wide,
  On four small wooden wheels;
Aunt Isa dresses him with flowers,
  And very pleased he feels.

For " Jack," he is a sturdy boy,
  Who does for ever stand,
Sheep-driving on our mantel-piece,
  ·With a long whip in hand.
When I won't kiss the folks, they say,
  " Then we'll kiss Jack instead,"
And I directly bend my will,
  By Jack's example led.

And " Mrs. Burr," she is my nurse,
  I beat her now and then,
But then she's really very kind,
  She never beats again.

Sidney! have you a "Burr?" and pray
  Does she not make you mind?
And cause your lordship to obey,
  Whene'er she feels inclined?

I on my father's shoulder ride,
  And pat his hat in glee;
He says he swung you there, but you
  Were not as pleased as me.
A giant you, a pigmy I,
  How different we must be!
And yet some day both stalwart men
  In us shall England see.

I'm sixteen months, you're five years old,
  Alas! we're not to meet;
But oh, be sure you send me now
  Some little answer sweet,
About your new and pleasant home,
  Your Malvern hills afar;
And if you can't write all yourself
  Ask help from your Mamma.

Mine bids me say, "that she has drawn
  Upon a page hard by,
My portrait,—I'm a daisy-bud,"
  No, surely, I'm a boy.
Sidney, I feel I am a boy,
  Born wild and bold and free;
You say, "you'll keep a toy-shop,"
  I say, "I'll go to sea."

And yet this would not sure fulfil,
  For each his mother's dreams;
They'd have us meet in College halls,
  And muse on nobler themes;
They love us with a mighty love,
  And so we ought to try
To be what they would have us be;
  Now, Sidney dear, good-by.

No. 6.

TO DEAR GRANDMAMMA AT D * * *.

WRITTEN AT RICHMOND.

Dear Grandmamma, I'm far away
  From my own home and you;
I'll write a line, I think, to-day
  To tell you how I do;
Or, as is more polite, enquire
  If all I left are well;
Yourself, and grandpapa, my aunts,
  " Poor Sam,"[1] and Isabel.

I find I've here an Uncle Sam,
  But gay, and bright, and tall,
I wonder he's not pale nor thin,
  Nor like *our* Sam at all.

[1] Recovering from illness.

My love to " Sam," I hope he'll go
  To Brighton's salt blue sea,
And grow, as here they say I grow,
  As fat as fat can be.

" Square, and well made for to be strong,"
  Of Norman Duke 'tis said,
Aunt Jane when reading this declared
  'Twould do for me instead ;
I'm glad I'm " strong," I hope some day
  Upon my arm you'll lean,
Dear grandmamma, as kindly yours
  Has oft borne me, I ween.

I shall not always pull and rend,
  Perchance as now I do ;
It seems I cannot keep my hands
  Off all things strange and new ;
Drawers, closets, and such pretty pipes,
  Around these rooms I see,
Made surely to take off and on,—
  A merry game for me.

Kind friends have various gifts bestow'd,
  I'm sure I thank them all ;
Aunt Jane a handsome box of bricks,
  And Uncle Sam a ball.
With pictures for my book, as well,
  Now pinn'd against the wall ;
Yet still dear " Toppie" bears the bell,
  The best beloved of all.

And on the water, in the boat,
  While swans come sailing by,
In the bright sunshine down we float,
  Papa, Mamma, and I.
The cows lie quiet on the bank,
  The crows career on high ;
Amongst all these you will believe
  Ernest 's a happy boy.

My love to Margaret and the flowers,
  I'll soon come back again,
When suns have dried the pelting showers,
  And ripe 's the golden grain.
I'll say no more, but now farewell,
  I'll write, I think I will,
Another letter soon. I am,
  Your loving Ernest still.

July, 1841.

No. 7.

TO AN AUNT AND UNCLE,

ON RECEIVING FROM THEM THE PRESENT OF A ROCKING-HORSE.

Dear Aunt and Uncle, your delightful note,
  Directed " Ernest R.," was well received,
From Richmond on the first of March you wrote
  (Oh, wondrous tale, which I with joy believed)

About a horse which down the Thames should float
  By the next barge.   Dear fellow, I am grieved
To say he has not yet beheld his master,
I wish those barges came a little faster.

But now the note—I think I'll try and write
  An answer whilst I wait; how very kind
To think of me, who long time " out of sight,"
  Might well have reckon'd to be " out of mind ";
My dear old " Rodney" sends his love—his state
  Is tolerable for his years.   You'll find
Whene'er at D * * * you like to come and see,
Papa, Mamma, my sister dear, and me.

                                    March 15. -
So far, dear Aunt, I scribbled, and the door
  Each knock, I hoped would open to the horse;
He came on Monday last, and not before.
  I was at dinner—hope had ceased, perforce
Of disappointment, day by day:—no more
  I ask'd for him, and then he came, of course,
Into the hall the noble creature rode,
And I ere long, his saddled back bestrode.

Into the hall he rode, nor tired, nor warm,
  His former grooms had for his welfare cared,
For straw and matting cased his agile form
  Enough to load a waggon.   So it fared;
Papa released him, and from wind and storm
  Securely housed, in snowy pride he reared

His mane and tail, and took his pleasant stall,
His place prepared, beside our nursery wall.

At first I must confess, I was afraid
  To rest in his bright stirrups, and to ride
Him fast, fast, fast! but now that fear is fled,
  'Tis a vast punishment to be denied
His use; and every morning when I've read
  And spelt, I long time on his back abide.
Dear Pegasus, I love him night and day,
Beautiful horse! oh, never go away!

Sweet Ada sits afar in wonder deep,
  Or claps her hands to see me prance along;
In at the window oft my uncles peep,
  Remembering the days when they were young;
They bid me canter on o'er hill and steep,
  And as I amble, I indite a song,
Unworthy but sincere, of thanks most true,
Kind Aunt and Uncle, for such gift to you.

1844.

TO ADA ON HER FIRST BIRTHDAY.

My little daughter,—come, sweet words
   And paint a portrait fair,
Of what she is at twelve months old,
   This little maiden rare.
She is—so doth her nurse declare,
She is—a child beyond compare.

Ada, my sunbeam, child of spring,
   Turn hither thy blue eyes,
Thou little winsome gleesome thing,
   What world of roguery lies
In thy demure and quiet seeming,
Oh Kitten! of what art thou dreaming?

What is it holds thee still and glad,
   Beneath the table hiding?
Some morsel sweet, of mischief sad
   For certain, is deciding;
Perchance to spring on Brother's tower,
And lay it level with the floor.

Come forth, a finger for thine aid—
   Another month by-gone,
Thy tiny feet, no more afraid,
   Shall bear thee all alone.

Proud of thy feats thou'lt pace along,
With a triumphant murmuring song.

I wonder if thy primal year
   Of life is omen true,
Of all thy future—Baby dear,
   We ask for thee anew,
This day the blessing of the Lord,
And seek to train thee by his word.

1844.

TO THE SAME,

ON HER SECOND BIRTHDAY.

ADA, thy second year hath flown,
   Thou bright and happy child;
Baby no longer, thou art grown,
   So wilful and so wild,
So meet to share thy brother's play,
Thou art more like him day by day.

Form'd to enjoy with fervid heart,
   High health and temper gay,
How rich the treasure that awaits,
   Possession for to-day.

A Baby-house, mine own, of yore,
To thee descends with all its store.

Its store, I mean, of memories old;
  Each room, and shelf, and floor,
Recall to me some childish dream,
  Some tale of nursery lore.
Yet not such joy to call it mine,
It was, as now, to see it thine.

Dolls, bricks and coaches, cast aside,
  Forgive the cold neglect!
Come, little mistress, in thy pride,
  The mansion's nooks inspect.
The kitchen and its pantry by,
Parlour and bedchamber on high.

A chest of drawers from foreign land,
  Tea-set, of English yew;
A stove, and crib, and washhand-stand,
  With bed of roseate hue.
How shall the treasures all be told,
Which love's kind hands for thee unfold?

One room for study, brother claims,
  His table and his chair;
His tiny folios with their names,
  Engross his learnèd care.
A clock—upon his mantel stands,
And points the time with mystic hands.
16

To thee he leaves the kitchen range,
    Fish-kettle, bread-tray, pail;
Each chair and sofa, thou canst change,
    And picture on its nail.
But only now and then presume,
To dust and tidy " Brother's room."

1845.

"JOHN HOLGATE."

THAT name! ah, forth will feeling gush,
　At its once pleasant sound;
A fount, where fresh and bitter tears,
　Are yet fast flowing found.
'Tis one of friendship's ruin'd shrines,
　And still she comes to keep,
Her mournful watch with memory there,
　To name that name and weep.

No seal of wasting pain was set
　On manhood's brow of pride!
Nor weight of years, nor hoary hairs,
　Were on him—that he died.
We think upon his guileless worth,
　His rich and lowly mind,
His warm and feeling heart, and hope
　Few more such friends to find.

In Him was true religion blent
　With intellect's high tone,

And meekly were the laurels worn,
    That ceaseless effort won!
Ah! who that mark'd his steady step,
    In traffic's arduous mart,
Had fancied his, the scholar's fame,
    And his, the poet's heart!

Our life wears on, the many meet
    Still in that house of prayer;
Alas! alas! his kindly smile,
    For ever missing there.
His little ones in sables veil'd,
    Fill up his vacant place!
And would ye know how he was loved,
    Look on their mother's face.

God of all grace! 'twas thine to still
    Their first wild bursts of grief;
Now dry the gushing tears that gave,
    Those broken hearts relief.
God of all love! their lonely home,
    With thy bright presence fill!
Thou hast cut off their staff and stay,
    Thyself be near them still.

Faith has an angel-arm, she lights
    A lamp within the tomb;
Pierces its awful solitudes!
    Unseals the narrow home!
"*He is not here!*" she cries, "why watch
    The graveclothes and the dust?

Forsake the sepulchre, and seek
   Far hence—the risen just.

" Up, mourner, where I point the way;
   Yon jasper wall behold!
Pass through the gates of pearl, and tread
   The streets of glassy gold.
There, where the crowns are casting down, · .
   And palms are waved in air,
And heaven's harps are ringing out,
   Behold him, *He is there!*

" That name, it is an angel's name
   In the Lamb's book of life;
See that thine own be there inscribed,
   End of the warrior's strife.
That name, it should have given birth
   To praise, and not despair;
To thoughts of heaven, and not of earth;
   Behold him, *He is there!*"

1838.

THE MOTHER'S LAMENT.

YES, tears must flow, and freely,
    Or bleeding hearts would break;
I love to watch this empty crib
    Though he's not here, to wake.
There is within my soul, a hope
    That wins it from despair;
I can look up to the bright sky
    And think that he is there;
But, my Willie, oh my Willie,
    My precious one, my pride,
As I turn to earth, and miss thee,
    I would thou hadst not died!
Thy favourite chair is vacant,
    Thy merry voice is hush'd,
And my bud, my plant of promise,
    In the quiet grave is crush'd.

There is a chasm in my heart,
    A vacuum and a void—
Somewhat, bound up with every nerve,
    Is sever'd and destroy'd;
Loved all too well; perchance, I own
    It help'd to make the nest
Of happiness below the skies
    Too soft—too meet for rest!

Now is the down all scatter'd wide
  Before the winds of heaven,
Lord! raise thine undivided throne
  In the chasm thou hast riven.
Thou sufferest not, that idols
  Should thy dominion share;
Thou hast made the world a wilderness,
  That it might not be a snare.

What was there given thee in that hour,
  My ransom'd one—my love!
Beyond the ken of babyhood,
  And mortal strength above?
Saw'st thou the Angel of the grave
  In gloomy garb flit by?
So would be cradled in the arms
  Of those thou lov'dst—to die?
Did th' infant pilgrim catch a glimpse,
  Of heaven's irradiate shore,
And deem earth's treasures after that
  As meet for him no more?[1]
What lines of glory broke the first
  Upon death's awful strife?
Thou'lt tell me when we meet again,
  Beside the stream of life.

Thy calm distinct " farewell," my child,
  I hear it o'er again;
'Tis mingled with the angels' hymns,
  Who waited for thee then.

[1] The child whispered to its father, " No more lambs, Papa."

Farewell, my darling—spread the wings
　　They teach thee to unfold;
I spare thee, love, to mount to heaven
　　On plumes of filmy gold.
Nor is thy mother left alone,
　　He who hath taken thee,
Will ever guide and comfort her
　　Across dark sorrow's sea.
From the children whom he chasteneth
　　He hideth not his face;
The tide of grief can never rise
　　Above the throne of grace.

I have many treasures left me,
　　Dark eyes are at my knee,
Gazing up into my face, with
　　Their serious sympathy.
The babe upon whose velvet cheek
　　Kisses and tears do meet,
Answers me ever with a smile,
　　Unconscious, calm and sweet.
And Thou, upon whose arm I lean
　　And every care repose;
In our garden is a cypress
　　Where there used to be a rose.
Its shadow chills us, but oh, still
　　Mercies are left to tell,
The hand of mercy planted *that;*
　　It hath done all things well.

1831.

"DEAD AND GONE."

SHE is dead! yes, she whom we loved is dead
She lies, as in sleep, on her quiet bed,
But she never has slept before as now—
'Tis a stony ear and an icy brow:
No answering smile, and no kindling eye,
Here is Death—in his peaceful majesty!
Of her whom we loved, we shall shortly say,
" Go, bury my dead, from my sight—to-day."

Thou dark King of terrors! howe'er thou appear,
We shiver to meet thee, in silence and fear,—
Solemn seal of our sin,—fulfilling the curse
('Mid groans of creation) which none may reverse.
One by one we go down to the gloom of the grave,
Till our glorious Deliverer, " mighty to save,"
Shall have conquer'd and won his inheritance vast,
Adding *Thee* to his trophies, O Death! at the last.

She is gone! yes, she whom we loved is gone,
The pall is lifted—the relics are borne
To their last long home and their kindred dust,
To abide, till the coming again of the just;
She entereth not at the opening door,
She graceth the family board no more,

We weep as we gaze on her vacant chair,
And the aching void we can hardly bear.

She is dead and gone! gone far away,
For the spirit is not with the buried clay;
Scarce a sigh attended its flight sublime,
When it rose and escaped from the trifles of time,—
No lengthen'd sickness—no conflict long,
Her hope was humble, her faith was strong;
In one silent night was the passage made,
And Jesus was with her—to solace and aid.

She is dead and gone! she is dead and gone!
In the darken'd house, on a Sabbath morn,
Her children mourn'd; while she, more blest,
To a wondrous reign of light and rest,
In angels' arms was carried on high,
Just as the murmurs came floating by,
From a thousand temples of praise and prayer,
To the courts above; she enter'd there.

She is gone—she is gone—from all earthly cares,
A spirit long dead to the world and its snares;
But living in Christ, and now caught to his side,
She patiently waits with the ransom'd, " the Bride:"
Till shortly her Lord to his kingdom shall come,
And his saints in their glorified bodies, the sum
Of immutable promise, shall reckon and reap,
And " to govern the nations," arise from their sleep.

Fare thee well, oh beloved! 'tis bitter to part!
Thou wert noble in mien—thou wert gentle in heart;
Thine age in its beauty remember'd shall be,
For life's reverend autumn was lovely in thee;
With the gold-tinted leaves from the earth thou hast past,
As corn in its season thou'rt garner'd at last;
Thy times are all told, of probation and pain,
And renew'd in thy youth, we shall meet thee again.

When those who have nurtured our earliest years
Depart—they must leave us in sables and tears;
Fresh footsteps will tread each familiar floor,
And the places that knew us shall know us no more;
Let a mother's sweet image, remember'd in love,
Now made like to her Lord in the mansions above,
Be our circlet of union, though scatter'd abroad,
Till we join her again in the presence of God.

" Yea, blessed the dead who have died in the Lord,"
Who have walk'd on the earth by the lamp of his word,
Whose light hath so shined with unvarying beam,
That glory through them hath been given to Him:
" Epistles of Christ," both in word and in deed,
Which the righteous have prized and the thoughtless may
      read,
They are gone—they are gone—to receive their reward;
Yea, blessed the dead who have died in the Lord.

1848.

THE FUNERAL AT SEA.

"Sad thoughts o'er memory sweep,
Whenever aught brings back that burial of the deep."

An Incident related in Captain Hall's Nautical Adventures.

FADING as fades the gather'd flower
    He wasted day by day;
'Twas not disease—it only seem'd
    Silent and slow decay;
Ill might such slight and fragile form
    Abide the ocean-storm.
Edwin, the perils of the sea
    Were never meant for thee!

All loved the boy;—he pined and died
    Far from his mother's side;
But the rough sailors on him smiled
    As on a petted child;
And manhood lent his sinking frame
    All aid its need might claim;
All loved to shield his drooping head,
    And watch his dying bed.

Dark night was o'er the sea, and loud
    The winter's wind did rave,
When we laid our little favourite
    In his deep ocean-grave.

Oh, mournfully the vessel's bell
   Toll'd out the funeral knell
That gather'd us around his bier;
   In every eye—a tear.

The ship was rocking in the blast,
   Chill fell the rain, and fast
On every head unshelter'd there;
   And on the book of prayer.
The whistling wind and rushing surge
   Mingled in fitting dirge,
But drown'd the solemn words they said
   Over the quiet dead.

The captain sign'd, the moment come
   To grant the greedy deep
One treasure more, till day of doom,
   In its vast caves to sleep.
We heard no plunge! such fearful gale
   Swept at that moment past,
It rent away the straining sail,
   And snapt the tottering mast.

Yet safe to port we rode! that storm
   By midnight's hour was o'er:
On its strong wing, *the sailors said*,
   That cherish'd form it bore
To rest, not in the waters cold,
   Nor sink in their caverns old;
For angel-wise—to him 'twas given
   To ascend on the storm to heaven.

ANNIE LANE.

" A COTTAGE TALE—O'ER TRUE."

BRIGHT-eyed child of six years old,
  Sweet little Annie Lane!
There she lieth! stiff and cold,
  Never to wake again.
Peace is on the infant brow,
All her moans are over now!

Quiet laid the little feet
  That ran at mother's word;
Or that, father's step to greet,
  Flew—as the sound she heard:
Shoes, new shoes, seem ready there,
Which those feet will never wear.

With thy basket trudging on,
  Thou 'lt be met no more;
Mother's biddings all are done,
  And every reckoning o'er.
None thro' all the dale could be,
Annie! miss'd so much as thee.

Weep! poor mother, thou *must* weep,
  Tho' all too weak for woe;

Soon thou shalt beside her sleep,
  Child and mother too.
And the blind, the helpless blind,—
Where shall father comfort find?

Yester-morn, upon his knee,
  With a most earnest mind,
Verse and verse she read with him
  Of gospel for the blind:
He with finger tracing,—she
Helping him so cheerily.

Then she laid her down to die,
  Smitten in one short hour;
All at once, and wearily,
  The pretty faded flower:
He placed the book beneath her head
For her waking—but she's dead.

Father's solace, mother's stay,
  Call'd home, as with a word;
They know WHO pluck'd the flower away,
  They know " it is the Lord."
The mother treads the Border-land,
Christ hath Annie in his hand.

*   *   *   *   *

Thy grave is just a fortnight old,
  Sweet little Annie Lane!
Again they raise the fresh-turn'd mould,
  The mourners wait again.

Dust to dust, beneath the sod,
Mother, too, is gone to God.

" Our Father" who hast blotted out
  The stars of the blind man's sky,
Amid his darkness, deep and lone,
  Still fix his heart on high.
Be Thou his sun, his shield, his stay,
And let him trust Thee, though Thou slay.

1854.

MARIE.

St. Aubyn's bay is sapphire bright,
  The deep still makes its moan
Around St. Helier's rocky height,
  And saintly cell of stone.
Light feet still tread that time-worn stair,
  Based in the ocean brine;
Bright eyes still beam whilst landing there,
  But Marie, where are thine?

Alas! alas! a quiet tomb
  In thy native isle is made;
And there in all thy youthful bloom
  Are thy bounding pulses laid.

So young! few knew what soul of fire
  From that fair dust hath fled,
Thy shroud enfolds thy modest lyre,
  And thou art with the dead.

A sister's eyes are dim with tears,
  Her tenderest guide is gone;
Light of thy father's widow'd years,
  How could'st thou leave him lone?
Sweet likeness of thy mother lost;
  Perchance a summons given
In her own angel tones thou heard'st,
  Bidding thee come to heaven.

No more, no more thy willing feet,
  The house of want shall seek;
No more, no more thy winning lips,
  The words of mercy speak.
I've seen the face of wither'd eld[1]
  Beam brightness at thy tread;
'Twill miss thee in its darksome home,
  For thou art with the dead!

Wild infancy and childhood own'd
  Through thee the Gospel's rule:
Rocks of Le Dicq, your rugged forms
  Witness'd the Sabbath school!
How week by week unweariedly
  That wild sea-path she trod,

[1] See "The Book and its Story," p. 359.
17

Thro' winter-storms and winds, to train
The uncultured mind for God.

Oh Marie! Marie! and on whom
    Thy mantle hast thou cast?
Thy lamp of unassuming love,
    Lit others as it past;
'Tis quench'd in Jordan's chilly wave,
    All brighter may they gleam;
For souls are hasting to the grave
    Without the Gospel's beam.

Let Jersey list her voice in death:
    " Dark France before us lies,
Her language ours,—our fleeting breath
    Must tell her ' Jesus dies.'
His death alone can save the lost!
    On, warriors, to the fight,
And if ye early fall like me,
    Ye win the crown of light.

" My father, sisters, mourn no more,
    Ye meet me soon above;
I and my brothers on that shore
    Abide through Jesu's love;
Here there is no more wasting pain,
    No ties asunder riven;
To live *was* Christ, to die was gain,—
    My kindred, come to heaven."

1839.

ON THE DEATH OF A FRIEND,

AGED SEVENTY-SIX.

Down to the shore of a dark stream there came
An aged man,—a man with silver hair:
Its cold waves kiss'd his feet, and his weak frame
Shook to its centre, with the chillness there:
He lean'd upon his staff as if in prayer,
Gazing across the flood,—then turn'd to bless
Those who were round him in the wilderness.

An old man's blessing and a patriarch's prayer,—
This rose to heaven, and that was softly shed
On all who reverently press'd to share
His last low words: on many a youthful head
They fell like Hermon's dews; and none need dread
Death's shadowy vale, if peace divinely beam
As thus, on either side the chilling stream.

The pilgrim waited, longing for the word
That bids the weary rest; and when 'twas given,
Pass'd joyfully to realms unseen, and heard
The welcome of his angel-guards to heaven,
Leaving his robes of clay in conflict riven,
Only from sorrowing friends erewhile to crave
A seemly folding for the quiet grave.

Then swell'd along the vale a mournful sound,
Low dirge-like voices met the moaning tide
Of such as wander'd near a funeral mound;
And opening its dark door, the grave replied,
" Here, with his household lay him side by side;
The calm remains are mine! and thus I claim
In years to come, whoever owns his name."

That silver head was seen by men no more:
Yet ere the solemn chamber closed, a ray
Fell from the skies upon its mouldering floor;
God, writing with a sunbeam, seem'd to say,
So its Redeemer shall reclaim this clay
At his last advent in eternal light,
To win the kingdoms of the grave, oh Night!

" Where are the fathers?" to our homes return'd;
One is gone from us to serener spheres;
We miss the light which long amongst us burn'd,—
Miss the sweet influence of those elder years.
Sorrow oft look'd on him and dried its tears;
And hope and joy have lost their kindly friend,
Whose temper'd age with each could bear and blend.

'Tis vacant space, yet still we seek him, where
He trimm'd his lamp for heaven in calm repose,
And turn to ask his counsel or his care;
Where,—far retired from vanities and shows,
He deeply drank of God's own word, and chose
From its rich armoury, oft a holy shield,
To gird some younger warrior for the field.

Youth link'd him in his rich autumnal prime
With many a fond conceit by fancy bred;
The father of the forest, touch'd by time,
Who to the earth inclined his honour'd head,
And his few branches as a shelter spread
To welcome woodland flower, and wilding spray,
Bright contrast to his beautiful decay.

The tree is fall'n—the sun is set, the tide,
Wave after wave has ebbed for ever now;
God bids the stream into the ocean glide,
We lose the light, we mourn the shade, yet bow
To sin's deep curse.   Since Jesus did endow
The grave as gate of life, and porch of bliss,
Let life's long day of trial end like this.

1836.

MUSINGS
BY THE GRAVE OF WORDSWORTH.

IN THE

"CHURCHYARD AMONG THE MOUNTAINS,"
GRASMERE.

FOUR peaceful babes in one eventful year
   First saw the light of day;
Napoleon, Turner, Wordsworth, Wellington:
   All now have pass'd away.
The Despot, Painter, Poet, Hero, each
   In his lone grave is laid:
Each had deep lesson to his race to teach
   Whose memory shall not fade.

Napoleon, firm of purpose, purposed ill,
   To make the world his slave;
Down trampled love and right, with selfish will,
   And found inglorious grave.
His blazing torch of conquest quench'd its light
   On a rock islet lone;
He scatter'd blight and death, and death and blight
   Fell on him, sire and son.

Prepared of God, as Britain's guide and guard
   Against that tyrant foe,
In war and peace, alike to watch and ward,
   Through half a century's flow,

Who e'er before exchanged like Wellington
  Laurel for olive crown?
Each nobly worn, as it was nobly won
  With a life-long renown!

His grateful country laid him to his rest
  With greater pomp than kings;
Princes to swell the solemn pageant prest;
  Europe his requiem sings.
In dim cathedral crypt his corse was shrined,
  And, as it sank from view,
Men said "that none like him was left behind,
  As England's foemen knew."

Those other babes were Spirits for the age
  Of peace the hero earn'd;
The Painter's skill transferr'd to magic page,
  The thoughts that in him burn'd.
Nature's bold pupil in her rarest moods,
  Master of mist and space;
He bade men seek her gorgeous solitudes,
  The truth he told to trace.

And here we stand beside the grassy mound,
  Where Wordsworth chose to lie;
Guarded by all the silent mountains round,
  And Rotha murmuring by;
Lough-rigg and Fair-field, watch towers of Grasmere,
  Seat-sandal, Silver-how,
Circle the ashes of their mighty seer,
  No more amongst them now.

Oh! He had ' lesson deep' the world to teach,
  From eighty quiet years,
Spent with these lights, these shadows, and these forms,
  Amid the rills and meres.
Their voices with his heart communed so long,
  We cannot choose but greet
Their echoes in his simple lofty song,
  Which gives them utterance meet!

Hath he not sent throughout his country's heart
  A love she scarcely knew,—
Or had forgotten amid schools of art,—
  For the simple and the true?
To God in Nature he hath bid men look,
  With deep and patient joy,
Observant, pore upon the mighty book,
  Spread forth for every eye.

Not in the picture mountain-land alone,
  Nor by the fair lake's side ;
But in a daisy's shadow he hath shown
  Reposeful thought may hide ;
That sunshine net-work on a brooklet's floor,
  A ripple and a gleam,
May scatter more than philosophic lore,
  The gloom of sorrow's dream.

Those other Three,[1] cathedrals crave their dust,
  And Wordsworth's craved the sod.
Know ye the wreathing, morning mountain mists,
  Like spirit-hosts abroad?

[1] Turner and Wellington are buried in St. Paul's ; Napoleon's remains
were brought from St. Helena to the Hotel des Invalides in Paris.

Oft fancy dreams them trains of pilgrim souls
   O'er tarn and fell that rove,
Who to this shrine bring offerings from afar,
   Of reverence and love.

He, who with God in Nature spent his life,
   Sought in its closing year,
To God in Christ, as with chastisèd heart,
   Resign'd, he sat him here.
Beneath these beeches, on this low stone wall,
   Where nothing speaks of gloom,
His earnest eye oft seem'd to penetrate
   The secrets of the tomb.

The precious daughter of his loving age
   Before him low was laid ;
" I am the Resurrection and the life,"
   To her had Jesus said ;
" In no wise will I him that comes cast out ; " [1]
   Words cheering her last hour ;
And thro' the daughter's solemn strength of faith,
   The father felt their power.

In foreign lands the yellow light that falls
   From a fair oriel pane,
Streams only on one massive tablet stone,
   Engraven " CHARLEMAGNE."

---

[1] These verses of Scripture are inscribed on Mrs. Quillinan's tombstone.

So here on this gray tablet of the hills
    Is " WILLIAM WORDSWORTH," all
That bids true lovers of the woods and rills
    Their mighty bard recall.

Deem'd we that sculpture, black with ages' gloom,
    Should grace the warrior dead?
That flowers, all lowly woodland flowers, should bloom
    Around the poet's bed?
Oh, no; art's richest pile had now grown gray,
    And, mouldering, taught alone
Charlemagne and his glory pass'd away,
    Like the recording stone.

And floral relics from our Wordsworth's grave,
    The daisy and its train,
So many eager worshippers would crave,
    That none would e'er remain.
The mighty genius of the hills appeals
    To Nature round him spread ;
She speaks his epitaph, and in *her* speech
    He lives, though he is dead.

1854.

The Six Days of Creatión. Illustrated with Eight
Steel Engravings. By W. G. Rhind. Third Edition, One volume,
square 12mo., cloth lettered, price 6s.

The Septuagint Greek Version, translated into
English, with Critical Notes. Two volumes, royal octavo, price 21s.

The Robin of Woodside Lodge : the Adventures
of a Robin; a true Tale. Eight coloured Engravings. 18mo., very neat.
Price 2s. 6d.

Bagster's Comprehensive Family, Pulpit, and
Study Bible, complete in one volume; with coloured maps, etc.
*The types used for the Text, the Notes, and References, have been
selected with special reference to easy legibility.*

The Treasury of Scripture Parallels. Price 10s.
cloth.

The Miniature Quarto Bible. Price 21s. 6d. cloth.
Handiness and legibility are the characteristics of this Bible.

THE "ENGLISH HEXAPLA":

The Greek Original of the New Testament Scrip-
tures, with the six principal English translations, arranged in parallel
columns beneath it. One volume quarto, price 2l. 2s.

Bishop Coverdale's First English Bible, quarto.
Price 30s. in cloth. With a portrait and facsimile title.

BAGSTER'S POCKET AND FACSIMILE LARGE-PRINT POLYGLOT BIBLES, AND CHURCH SERVICES.

THESE elegant Bibles and Church Services are printed of three different
sizes of exactly uniform arrangement, so that the pages of each, though
differing as to size of type, exactly correspond, line for line and word
for word. The Bibles are kept bound up with the Common Prayer,
Indexes, Concordances, etc., and with various languages, Hebrew, Greek,
Latin, etc., page for page.

Catalogues gratis. By post, free.